# TRUE CRIME :
# MICHIGAN

## The State's Most Notorious Criminal Cases

### Tobin T. Buhk

D1599958

# STACKPOLE
# BOOKS

0  11557 00713  8

Published by
STACKPOLE BOOKS
5067 Ritter Road
Mechanicsburg, PA 17055
www.stackpolebooks.com

Printed in the United States of America

10  9  8  7  6  5  4  3  2

FIRST EDITION

Cover design by Tessa J. Sweigert

Cover photos: Prescription bottle with poison caution, ©Mike Flippo/Shutterstock; Suspected Purple Gang members using their hats for cover, *Detroit News*; Grand Rapids serial killer Martha Beck after her confession, evidence in a suitcase belonging to the Lonely Hearts killers, Raymond Fernandez describing his crimes during a lengthy confession, and Michigan police inspecting the cement grave of a murder victim buried in a cellar, Grand Rapids History & Special Collections, Archives, Grand Rapids Public Library, Grand Rapids, MI; police discover an illegal brewery in Prohibition-era Detroit, National Archives and Records Administration; one of the many notes issued by private banks during the Wildcat era, Tobin T. Buhk; disposing illegal alcohol during Prohibition, Library of Congress, Prints and Photographs Division, NYWT&S Collection.

**Library of Congress Cataloging-in-Publication Data**

Buhk, Tobin T.
  True crime : Michigan : the state's most notorious criminal cases / Tobin T. Buhk. — 1st ed.
      p. cm.
  Includes bibliographical references.
  ISBN-13: 978-0-8117-0713-8 (pbk.)
  ISBN-10: 0-8117-0713-X (pbk.)
  1. Crime—Michigan—History. 2. Crime—Michigan—Case studies. 3. Michigan—History. I. Title.
  HV6793.M5B84 2011
  364.109774—dc22
                                    2011001930

# Contents

# CHAPTER 1

# A Brief History of
# Crime in Michigan

The first chapter of Michigan's criminal history was written before Congress made it the twenty-sixth state in 1837. According to some early Michigan chroniclers, the Great Lakes State became United States property in part because of the crimes that took place in what is now Michigan.

Much of Michigan's bloody past centered on its largest permanent settlement—a fur-trading depot named Fort Detroit. The town also became infamous as the murder capital of the Midwest. Just hearing the name "Detroit" sent shivers down the spines of pioneers throughout the area.

If Detroit had a bad rep, much of it was earned under the guidance of Lt. Gov. Henry Hamilton—"The Great Hair Buyer of Detroit"—and his chief justice, Philippe DeJean.

At the onset of the American Revolution, Detroit was under British rule. When war broke out, British authorities feared that western settlers would rush to the aid of the eastern colonists. Aware of Detroit's strategic value as the gateway to the west, they worried that the area's pro-American settlers would loosen the British grip on the Midwest or even pull their hands off of it entirely. To protect their assets in the Midwest, the British enlisted the aid of Indian tribes, inciting them to wage war on American settlements with a threat that hit close to home: If the Americans win, they will take your hunting grounds. The British knew that this war strategy would lead to the murder of innocent civilians, but they followed it anyway.

While the documentary evidence—correspondence and diary entries—tends to be heavily biased toward one side or the other, one thing remains clear: There was a great deal of bloodletting in the Midwest, and Detroit under Henry Hamilton was at the center of it.

Captain Henry Hamilton became lieutenant governor of Detroit in 1775, and he immediately began to organize war parties. He established good relations with the area's native groups, but he was also ordered to recruit them to England's war against the colonists. So Fort Detroit became the launching point for raids against colonial settlements in Kentucky and Ohio.

From Hamilton's letters, it becomes clear that he acknowledges the possibility of collateral damage. In a letter dated April 1778, he explains the need to keep the killing to a minimum. The war parties must "act with humanity," he says, so all can live in peace "when His Majesty shall be pleased to order the hatchet to be buried."

Until that time, it was Hamilton's job to place the hatchet in the hands of his allies. Before war parties commenced, a ritual took place during which the governor passed a tomahawk to the head of the war party—a gesture to say that the two groups held the handle together in their war against the Americans.

This ceremony was more than a gesture. Hamilton placed the war parties under the direct leadership of British and French Canadians fighting for the British (some sources say to minimize the killing), but many of these leaders had questionable reputations. Although Hamilton wrote about keeping the carnage under control, these war parties murdered many innocent civilians, including women and children.

As an incentive, Hamilton allegedly offered $5 for each scalp brought to him. Most historians consider this nothing more than a legend, but the story spread throughout the Northwest Territory, and Henry Hamilton became known as "The Great Hair Buyer" or the "Hair Buyer General of Detroit." Pioneers despised him.

Although no documentary evidence exists to prove that the Hair Buyer offered bounties for scalps, according to nineteenth-century historian Silas Farmer, "The fact is undoubted and indisputable that at Detroit and other posts under both French and English rule, the Indians received goods in payment for human scalps as regularly as for coon and muskrat skins." Trading posts regularly stocked and sold scalping knives. Supposedly, a sign posted in front of a merchant's store on what is now Jefferson Avenue advertised "Scalping knives for sale here."

Some sources have Hamilton paying higher bounties for prisoners in an attempt to encourage the taking of captives and therefore lessening the bloodshed. If true, it didn't work. The war parties returned to Detroit with more scalps than captives. Even Hamilton acknowledged this fact. In a letter to Gen. Guy Carleton dated January 15, 1778, Governor Hamilton states that the war parties brought in twenty-three prisoners and one hundred and twenty-nine scalps. In another letter to Carleton dated September 17, 1778, Hamilton notes that in the four months since May, war parties entered Detroit with a total of thirty-four prisoners and eighty-one scalps.

Letters and journals of colonial residents describe bloodcurdling tales of captives beaten throughout the streets of Detroit, but the prisoners who did make it to Fort Detroit alive were not always treated as harshly as some contemporary sources suggest. In fact, Hamilton had a reputation for being an excellent host to captured American prisoners. Daniel Boone, who did a stint as a prisoner in Fort Detroit, spoke kindly of his British jailor.

As ruthless as the raids sanctioned by Hamilton may have been, it was the lawless element inside Fort Detroit that led to his downfall. Even in its earliest days, the fur-trading settlement was victimized by a steady crime rate. Robbery and murder took place often. Eager to keep the peace, British colonial authorities inflicted harsh penalties on criminals.

During Henry Hamilton's time as lieutenant governor, Detroit had its own hanging judge—a ruthless man named Philippe DeJean, who often exceeded his authority in punishing lawbreakers. DeJean sentenced offenders to death even though he didn't have the authority to do so, and Hamilton supported his decisions. One incident was so flagrant that it would lead to criminal indictments against both DeJean and Hamilton.

A man named Jean Contencineau, who worked for the settlement's largest trading post, robbed his employer with the help of a slave named Anne Wyley. The two stole some furs and the cashbox from the storehouse before setting it on fire. When caught, they immediately confessed, each one pointing the finger at the other.

DeJean sentenced both to hang, but the citizens of Detroit were enraged with his decision that such a petty offense like robbery warranted the death penalty. No one wanted to participate in the execution, so DeJean offered Wyley a deal—a pardon in exchange for hanging her co-conspirator. She took the deal but botched the hanging. Contencineau died a slow, agonizing death by strangulation. Later, DeJean went back on the deal and had Wyley hanged.

It was the last straw. The citizens of Detroit had had enough of Henry Hamilton and Philippe DeJean. The people complained to the authorities in Montreal, who indicted both for "acting illegally" in inflicting such harsh penalties on lawbreakers. But fate had something else in store.

American George Rogers Clark had taken Vincennes, Indiana, and the British feared that he could use it as a base to launch an attack against Fort Detroit. Hamilton decided to march on Vincennes in an attempt to reclaim the area from Clark's forces.

In October 1778, Hamilton left Detroit and led his army to Vincennes. He managed to recapture the frontier post from a skeleton crew left behind by Clark but then lost it again when Clark's army returned. During the scuffle, both Hamilton and DeJean were captured and treated more like war criminals than prisoners of war. Inflamed settlers wanted to hang Hamilton and his corrupt chief justice, but the duo was sent to Williamsburg, Virginia, instead. They were found guilty of committing war crimes and thrown in the Williamsburg dungeon, where they were kept in chains.

Colonel Arendt Schuyler DePeyster—a Tory from New York—replaced Hamilton. Under the new governor, the war parties continued to gather in Detroit. Like Hamilton, DePeyster may have tried to minimize the bloodletting, but the slaughter of innocent settlers continued and may have even escalated. According to one estimate, during the latter days of the Revolution, some three thousand people lost their scalps.

In 1783, the British declared an end to hostilities, and a year later, the Treaty of Paris made it official. In the decade following the treaty, a few skirmishes took place in the Northwest Territory, but with the signing of the Jay Treaty in 1796, the British surrendered their frontier forts to the United States, including Fort Detroit.

As for Hamilton, after a few years in the Virginia dungeon, he was set free and went on to become Lieutenant-Governor of Canada and later Governor of Bermuda. Whether or not he bought scalps or promoted the wanton slaughter of innocent settlers, Hamilton enjoyed a successful career as a British colonial governor.

Philippe DeJean, who was released from prison after serving four months, faded into obscurity. He did not immediately return to Detroit out of fear that he would face prosecution, but it appears that he did later join his family there.

The story of "The Hair Buyer General" and his chief justice has an interesting postscript. During the treaty talks that ended the war, the Revolutionaries staked their claim to Detroit and the territory that would later become Michigan in part on the capture of Henry

Hamilton. According to early Detroit historian Clarence Burton, "the consequences" of Hamilton's capture "were that Michigan, Ohio, Indiana, Illinois, and Wisconsin became a part of the new United States . . . by right of conquest."

According to Burton's version of events, when Clark took Vincennes, Hamilton recognized an opportunity to kill two birds with one stone. He could flee Detroit and the indictment pending against him, handed down in part because of the Contencineau case, and at the same time save face with the British colonial authorities by recapturing the outpost. But Clark captured Hamilton instead, which led to the "right of conquest" claim during later negotiations. Burton concludes that "to the blood of Jean Contencineau we owe, in part at least, the fact that we are citizens of Michigan." In other words, Michigan partly resulted from the unjust hanging of a thief.

With the war behind them, settlers enjoyed a brief period of peace in the newly formed Michigan Territory. They had just enough time to take a breath, because a few years later, the United States was back at war with the British.

The War of 1812 brought a new wave of atrocities. The most infamous incident—the River Raisin Massacre—occurred near present-day Monroe in southeastern Michigan.

In January 1813, a force of Kentuckians attacked Frenchtown, which was under the control of the British and their Indian allies. After some fierce fighting, the defenders fled with the Kentuckians in hot pursuit. When the Kentuckians caught up with them, they killed and scalped several Indians. Victorious, the Kentuckians returned to Frenchtown, where the officers enjoyed the town's supply of liquor and went on a bender.

The officers didn't anticipate the British counterattack, which left the American forces scattered and in chaos. Four hundred Kentuckians managed to hold the stockade until they were informed that their commanding officer, who had been taken prisoner, had surrendered the fort. The angry Kentuckians agreed to leave on one condition: a promise that their wounded would not be harmed. The British general gave his word. The Kentuckians threw down their weapons in disgust and marched out of Frenchtown as British captives.

Afraid of a counterattack, the British left behind eighty wounded Americans, mostly Kentuckians, with the promise that they would send help for them the next day. The next morning arrived, and a group of inebriated Indians showed up instead. They shot and scalped some of the wounded men and set fire to the homes that housed the others. When the men tried to jump out of the windows, the Indians beat them and pushed them back into the flames. In all, the Indians executed an estimated sixty men, taking the rest as prisoners, some of whom were ransomed in Detroit. News of the atrocity spread through the American forces, and when the British suffered a decisive loss nine months later, the Americans shouted "Remember the Raisin."

By 1814, hostilities once again came to an end, this time for good. With war finally behind them, settlers could return to farming. Even in times of peace, though, Michigan territory was a rough place. Traveling from one place to another came with great risk; bandits would rob passersby and then disappear into the thick forests. To deter highway robbery and provide travelers with safe havens, chains of inns and taverns with colorful names like the Black Horse Tavern were placed at regular intervals along major roads.

Once again, Detroit became the state's criminal capital. Eager to keep the peace, city officials passed stricter laws. Taverns had to purchase liquor licenses and could not sell alcohol on Sunday, except to travelers, and gambling was made illegal in places that sold liquor.

These protective measures didn't work. People bypassed the laws by selling liquor out of their homes, even on Sunday. As a result, Detroit had a real wild side in the early days of the Michigan Territory. Drunks ambled about the streets. Fights, murder, and robbery became common. The city fined those guilty of disorderly conduct, but most offenders couldn't pay the $3 to $10 fine. So they paid their debt to society by doing community service. For more serious offenses, such as unpaid debt, petty theft, repeated brawling, or spousal abuse, criminals were publicly flogged at the city's whipping post. A typical sentence consisted of thirty-nine lashes.

Although early Michigan lacked a hanging judge like DeJean, individuals found guilty of murder were periodically sentenced to death by hanging. These executions failed to deter criminals and were not popular among citizens. One infamous case created such a backlash that the death penalty was abolished in Michigan.

Stephen G. Simmons ran a tavern in Wayne County. With a massive build, Simmons was an intimidating figure who became violent when he drank. On several occasions, the burly barkeep picked fights with his customers. He had a sickly wife and two daughters, who lived in constant fear of their father's violent temper. One night in 1830, they witnessed a tragic scene.

Simmons burst into the bedroom with a jug of whiskey and demanded that his wife drink with him. She took a few sips and handed the jug back to her inebriated husband. When he demanded that she drink more, she refused, so he leveled her with a single, powerful punch. His daughters tried to stop him, but it was too late. His wife lay dead on the floor.

The Simmons trial rocked the community. Simmons was an educated, handsome man. He didn't look like a degenerate, and people found it hard to believe that whiskey turned this Jekyll into a Hyde. That is, until they heard from his daughters.

The Simmons girls testified against their father and told sordid stories of drunken binges when Simmons would take out his rage on them and their mother. Simmons was found guilty and sentenced to death by hanging.

Even though Simmons proved to be a fiend, the trial created a deep rift in the community. His death sentence caused an outcry throughout the area. The very idea of public execution was debated on the floors of the area's taverns and saloons. No one wanted to do the hangman's job, which must have seemed like déjà vu to the city residents who were old enough to remember the name Jean Contencineau. The Wayne County sheriff refused to participate. But "Uncle Ben" Woodworth, who owned the Steamboat Hotel, believed in strict enforcement of the law and volunteered to do the honors. He was appointed acting Sheriff of Wayne County so he could serve as hangman.

A large crowd, including many of Simmons's enemies, gathered to watch justice in action. Uncle Ben waited on the gallows while Simmons gave an eloquent speech to the crowd. He spoke about the evils of liquor and pleaded for mercy. Then to everyone's amazement, he began singing a hymn in his deep, baritone voice. The crowd had come to celebrate justice, but Simmons's singing changed the mood entirely. Even his enemies—men who had tangled with Simmons in one of his drunken brawls—began to feel sorry for the condemned man. A few seconds later, Simmons was dead.

And so was the death penalty in Michigan. The execution affected lawmakers, who did away with the infamous whipping post and abolished capital punishment. To this day, Michigan is one of the few states that do not legally permit executions.

In 1837, Michigan territory finally became a state. That same year, the legislators of the new state became unintentional accomplices in one of history's largest scams when they passed the General Banking Law—the first state in the Union to pass what became known as a free-banking law. The new law gave rise to bunco and counterfeiting on a statewide scale.

Under the General Banking Law, any group of twelve or more landowners was allowed to open a bank if it had capital of at least $50,000 and enough gold or silver to back thirty percent of its assets. The law also allowed banks to print and issue their own paper money, which was redeemable in gold or silver upon demand.

This situation led to all sorts of underhanded business and schemes. Banks would share capital and transport gold from one bank to another just in time for the arrival of the inspectors. And with very few eyes watching them, the bankers issued far more banknotes than they had assets to cover. This worthless paper money flooded the state, leaving many a merchant with a fistful of paper he could exchange for gold, if the issuing bank had any gold, and if the merchant could even find the bank.

To protect their scam and ensure a profit, some banks made it almost impossible for their customers to redeem the notes they issued. They issued the banknotes in one place but made them redeemable only in another, usually a remote place—in the middle of the woods or on the other side of the state. These places were as hard to find as wildcats, giving these banks the nickname "wildcat banks." Banks popped up anywhere and everywhere—in the backroom of a saloon, a shack in the middle of the woods, and according to one story, inside a tree stump.

This bizarre system also gave rise to gangs of counterfeiters and forgers who decided they could cash in on the thousands of banknote types floating around. They altered or raised (changed a $10 bill to a $100) notes and in some cases even created their own and attempted to pass them off as legitimate. One enterprising group stole notes printed for a bank that never opened—the Bank of Romeo—and used the bills to defraud citizens. Later, forgers altered the notes by scraping of the "o" in "Romeo" and attempted to use them in New York as legitimate notes from the Farmers Bank of Rome.

Eventually, the notes of even legitimate banks became worthless when merchants refused to take them. The state legislature decided to end the madness by suspending the General Banking Law a year later in 1838. Overnight, the wildcat banks folded, but the damage had been done. Legitimate banks folded alongside illegitimate ones—innocent victims of this statewide bunco scheme. Customers of legitimate banks stood to lose their assets until the state supreme court made a series of rulings that prevented people from losing everything, including their homes.

As Michigan grew, so did its crime rate. The expansion of the railroads in the 1850s opened up the north for miners and lumberjacks who built temporary logging camps. By day, they worked the virgin forests of northern Michigan, and by night, they played in the innumerable saloons and brothels that sprang up around their camps. Inevitably, there was mayhem.

Most of these fights were not settled in courtrooms but in barrooms by the strongest and meanest, or by a judge who heard arguments in between shots of whiskey. This frontier justice wasn't always just, but it worked. Nevertheless, it couldn't stem the tide of lawlessness that characterized this Wild West of Michigan.

One humorous incident of this lumberjack law occurred in the small town of Edenville. The town's saloons and hotels hosted thirsty lumberjacks who worked the forests of central Michigan from nearby Camp 16 and used the Tittabawassee River to move the logs. Edenville became sin central with places like Swearin' Charlie Axford's Hotel and the Red Keg Saloon at the center of the action.

Billy McCrary, the owner of the Red Keg, scuffled with a customer and beat the man senseless. The town constable immediately arrested McCrary, but when Swearin' Charlie Axford saw the arrest, he said there was no need to bother the justice of the peace; he could hold court. The constable agreed.

During the "trial," McCrary admitted his guilt, and "Judge" Axford handed down the sentence: a fine of $3 and a round of drinks for everyone at the Red Keg. After McCrary paid his debt, Axford decided to use the $3 fine to buy as many drinks as it would. McCrary paid for his crime while making a few dollars, and the injured man drowned his pain with several shots of whiskey. Everybody won and justice—frontier justice—was served.

Change the names and this scene could have occurred in several places throughout the state. As rough as these logging camps were, though, they were tame compared with the wild, wild west of Michigan's Upper Peninsula, where outlaws and tin stars dueled with hot lead and thirsty lumberjacks partied in Helltown, USA.

There were professional peacekeepers in Michigan at the time, although the sheriffs designated to keep the peace were outmanned, overworked, and in some cases as ruthless as the criminals. Contemporary tourists who visit the ghost town of Aral can still see the infamous Hanging Tree of Aral, which was the site of a fascinating story of frontier justice.

Charlie Wright operated a lumber mill in the town of Aral along Lake Michigan's northeastern coast in Benzie County. He was highly successful and popular among locals, but he did have one flaw: He became violent when he drank, which was often. In 1889, Wright feuded with local authorities over a tax issue. When Sheriff A. B. Case sent two deputies to serve a writ, they found him waiting with a rifle and a bottle of whiskey. The meeting turned into a skirmish and Wright shot both men.

The two deputies that Wright murdered were very popular, and soon a lynch mob formed at Wright's mill. Sheriff Case had to find Wright before the mob did, so he turned to the hanging tree, a tall white pine. He strung up one of Wright's workers and told the man to shake his legs when he felt like talking. It didn't take long. Case found Wright before the mob and managed to deliver him alive for trial in a real court. Wright received two life sentences for the murder of the two deputies. The hanging tree saved Wright from hanging at the expense of an innocent man.

And this was just the beginning of Michigan's criminal history—a fascinating book with blood-spattered pages.

# CHAPTER 2

# Strang Circumstances: The Murder of Michigan's Beaver Island King

Michigan once had a king. James Jesse Strang's kingdom consisted of Beaver Island—at fifty-eight square miles, the largest island in Lake Michigan. His subjects, who called themselves Strangites, crowned him king in 1850. King James governed his subjects with a strict set of rules, sometimes inflicting harsh punishments on those who disobeyed. Strang sidestepped many attempts, including one by the United States government, to tear down his empire. But he couldn't dodge assassins' bullets.

The future king of Beaver Island grew up on a farm in north-central New York. James Jesse Strang was born on March 21, 1813, the second of three children. A sickly child who attended school only until the age of twelve, Strang had a keen intelligence and a quick wit. He mastered the writings of Thomas Paine and early philosophers. As a teenager, he also kept a diary, part of which he wrote in an elaborate code.

Strang's visions of grandeur began to appear at an early age. In his journal, he expressed his desire to achieve greatness like Caesar or Napoleon. "My mind has always been filled with dreams of royalty and power," Strang wrote. But by nineteen, he hadn't yet reached his lofty goal of becoming a famous general or statesman.

Strang's ambition led him to ponder a wedding to England's twelve-year-old Queen Victoria. He discusses the possibility in his diary, but Victoria wed a few years later, in 1840, leaving Strang without the kingdom or the prominence he so desperately wanted. He did eventually get married, but not to a queen; he wed a Baptist minister's daughter named Mary Perce.

Dissatisfied with the mundane life of routine and chores on the farm, Strang went to law school. He earned a degree and traveled to Wisconsin Territory, where he opened a practice. Strang's sharp wit served him well in his legal practice, and he often argued the finest points of law. He once represented one neighbor who sued another over honey stolen by the neighbor's bees.

In 1844, thirty-one-year-old Strang heard about Mormon prophet Joseph Smith Jr. He traveled to the Mormon mecca of Nauvoo, Illinois, to meet the mysterious man. Impressed, Strang converted and became an elder in Smith's church. Strang then returned to Wisconsin Territory, where he agreed to open a Mormon colony in the vicinity of Burlington.

A few months after Strang's conversion, on June 27, a lynch mob stormed the jail in Carthage, Illinois, where Joseph Smith and his brother Hyrum were being held on charges of inciting riot and treason. The mob murdered both men, leaving the Mormons without a leader. An internal power struggle followed between Brigham Young, Sidney Rigdon, and James Strang.

Strang bolstered his claim to the Mormon throne with a letter signed by Joseph Smith and dated eight days before his assassination. The letter bears a Nauvoo postmark of June 18, 1844—days before Smith's murder—but some modern scholars believe that Smith's signature is a forgery.

In the letter, Joseph Smith describes a vision in which God told him that Strang would "plant a stake of Zion in Wisconsin"—a city called Voree. The letter also says that should anything happen to Smith, Strang should take over as the Mormon leader. Strang also told his followers that an angel had visited him and appointed him as Smith's rightful successor.

Despite the letter and the nod from a visiting angel, Brigham Young won the power struggle. The Twelve Apostles excommunicated both Rigdon and Strang, but the feud caused a fracture among the Mormon faithful. A majority followed Young to Utah, but a significant number followed Strang to Wisconsin.

Strang would not disappoint them. In 1845, he told his followers that he had received a vision: God said that he would give Strang access to ancient tablets and the means to translate them. Strang, it appeared, had followed in the footsteps of Joseph Smith.

Years earlier, Smith had told his followers that he experienced a similar miracle when an angel named Moroni visited him and gave him access to golden plates and two stones called Urim and Thummim for translating the plates. Smith took a few followers into the woods, where Moroni appeared and showed them the plates.

The plates told the story of the Nephites, a group from Palestine who settled in North America before the time of Christ. A battle nearly wiped out the Nephites, but Moroni managed to survive. He safeguarded the plates, which his father Mormon wrote and he finished, by burying them. With the Urim and Thummim, Smith translated the tablets. The text became the Book of Mormon, which formed the basis for Smith's new church.

Like Smith, it appeared Strang would receive help from a divine source. A few months after his vision of God, according to Strang, an angel gave him the Urim and Thummim and pointed out the spot where Strang could find the ancient tablets mentioned in his vision. Guided by the angel's directions, Strang led four followers to an oak tree on the Hill of Promise outside Voree. The men unearthed a canister containing three plates written in a strange, unknown language. Strang translated the plates, which he said were written by a Nephite survivor named Rajah Manchou. The plates alluded to Strang's rightful place at the head of the Mormon tabernacle.

Along with the miracle of the Rajah Manchou plates, Strang provided his people with a pleasant alternative to the polygamy favored by Brigham Young's group. He was an outspoken critic of plural marriage and a proponent of monogamy. But then in 1849, he apparently had a change of heart.

Strang's personal secretary, the mysterious Charles J. Douglas, first appeared in September 1849. The boy went everywhere Strang went. When Strang spoke, Charles stood by his side. They appeared close—very close—too close for some, and the rumors began to fly.

Charles was really Elvira Eliza Field, Strang's nineteen-year-old bride and second wife. Strang married Field in 1849 and kept the fact secret until the Kingdom of Strang could be established. To keep up the ruse, Elvira cropped her hair and wore men's clothes. When Strang unveiled his new bride about a year after their clandestine wedding, the news rocked the Strangite community. Despite Strang's rhetoric and the fact that he practiced what he preached (he eventually married five women), his new stance on plural marriage would later cost him many of his followers, including his first wife, Mary.

While Elvira masqueraded as Charles, Strang's kingdom was under construction in Michigan. In 1848, he led his flock to the new location. Strang told his followers that he experienced a vision of where the Strangites should settle. That place would be Beaver Island.

It is uncertain why Strang chose the large, sandy island in Lake Michigan for his kingdom. Some speculate that he passed the island during a trip down the lake and liked what he saw. Others believe that he wanted to build his utopia in an isolated place, far from the outside world and with enough land for all of his followers.

In 1848, Beaver Island had plenty of both. The land was cheap, at about $1.25 an acre. Apart from a few fishing villages and a few dozen Chippewa families, the island about twenty miles away from mainland Michigan was largely unpopulated. It also had a natural harbor, which local sailors called Paradise Bay, and an abundance of valuable timber.

A significant number of Strangites followed their leader and settled on Beaver Island. They established a town called St. James, after their soon-to-be king, and on July 8, 1850, they held a formal coronation. About two hundred Strangites witnessed the crowning. Strang sat, center stage, on a throne. He wore a red flannel robe and held a wooden scepter. His right-hand man, a former Shakespearean actor named George J. Adams, placed a paper crown decorated with stars on Strang's head. James Jesse Strang was now King James I.

Under Strang, the Mormons began to develop Beaver Island. They conducted a scientific survey of the island, built roads, and even established the the first newspaper in northern Michigan, the *Northern Islander.*

But from the start, Strang's kingdom was dogged by accusations and fighting with the island's gentiles. Strang never declared himself king of anything except his church, but the Strangites controlled Beaver Island and imposed their laws—Strang's laws—on the gentiles, who resented the man they came to see as the island dictator.

The area's non-Mormon population distrusted Strang's people. When a fishing boat or net went missing, the finger of blame always seemed to point at the Strangites. When the teetotaling Strang banned the sale of liquor on Beaver Island, levying fines so steep that no one could pay them, gentiles accused the Strangites of using the ban as an excuse to board ships, enter houses, and rifle through shops to seize contraband. King James was himself the subject of an allegation that he imposed high property taxes in order to swindle land around St. James and Paradise Bay.

The law attempted to net Strang by arresting him for an alleged threat against Louisa Adams, the wife of the man who crowned him. Strang said that Louisa tried to slander his name when she spread rumors that he lusted after the fifteen-year-old daughter of a subject named Franklin Johnson. Strang had her and her husband excommunicated, but George Adams told authorities that Strang pushed her off Beaver Island by threatening her life. Strang spent a few days in jail and then returned to his kingdom.

Strang dodged a bullet, but the real trouble was on its way. Tales of alleged crimes committed by the Strangites reached all the way to Washington, causing President Millard Fillmore to order an investigation in 1851.

The U.S. government sent a warship, the *Michigan*, to Beaver Island to apprehend the Mormon king. The allegations included counterfeiting coins, theft, treason, and trespassing on government lands—a charge brought because the Strangites removed wood from Beaver Island without government permission.

The Strangites prevailed in court and in the nation's newspapers, and Strang enjoyed a newfound popularity. In a stunning twist, he won a seat to the Michigan State Legislature. He was an efficient legislator, giving eloquent and persuasive speeches. Five of the bills he introduced passed into law, and his peers considered him one of the best debaters on the floor. He won re-election in 1855 and eyed the governor's office, but he would not have the chance to run. Trouble was brewing back on Beaver Island.

Strang had fended off attacks from angry gentiles and even the U.S. government, but his kingdom faced the biggest threat from within. During the winter of 1856, a small group of Strang's subjects, led by Thomas Bedford, began to conspire against their ruler. The seeds of Bedford's discontent were sown earlier, oddly enough, when Strang imposed a dress code on his female subjects.

In 1855, King James decided that women should wear short (to the knees) rather than long (to the ankles or the floor) dresses with matching bloomers underneath. He announced the dictate at a church meeting and added that women who did not obey his orders would be disciplined.

This new style would be less cumbersome than the massive hoop skirts considered fashionable at the time. And by the time Strang ordered the dress, many of Beaver Island's female residents had already adopted the new style, which suited the rugged landscape better than a ball gown. But the women accustomed to long skirts did not like the new look. Social customs of the time put men in pants and women in skirts. Perhaps the ladies felt that this new dress was too masculine, or perhaps they didn't want others to see their legs, albeit covered by baggy pants.

The wives of four future conspirators—Thomas Bedford, Alexander Wentworth, Hezekiah D. MacCulloch, and Franklin Johnson—did not follow Strang's new dress code. They paid the price, particularly Bedford. Mormon leadership targeted Bedford with liens against his property. Bedford also claimed that many fellow Mormons refused to pay him money they owed and stole some of his property.

The angry Bedford began to tell everyone and anyone who would listen about alleged Mormon thefts on a neighboring island. Strang could not tolerate what amounted to sedition. One night in April, a group of Mormons summoned Bedford to the printing office. They told him that the Mormon leadership had sentenced him to thirty-nine lashes for making false allegations. Another version of events has Bedford lashed for adultery.

Whatever the reason, Bedford received thirty-nine strokes with a horsewhip and wood switches. The punishment didn't injure him severely—he was allowed to keep his shirt on—but nonetheless, it cut him deeply. Bedford had endured what he considered harassment and now a beating. Strang wasn't present at the flogging, but Bedford believed the king ordered it. So he decided to murder Strang.

Bedford found a willing accomplice in Alexander Wentworth. Apparently, he had a disagreement with Strang about polygamy. There may have been another reason as well. There was some speculation that Strang wanted to marry Wentworth's sweetheart—Franklin Johnson's daughter Phebe (who ultimately married Wentworth). Motivated by a personal grudge, Wentworth began to conspire with Bedford and MacCulloch to rid themselves of their overbearing leader.

MacCulloch, like Wentworth, was a loyal subject and even an elder under Strang. But he disregarded the Mormon precept of temperance. MacCulloch drank heavily, often tipping a few onboard ships that stopped at Beaver for wood. According to some, MacCulloch also tipped the scales in his favor, using a golden thumb when weighing product. Amid rumors of Bedford's underhanded and fraudulent business practices, Strang excommunicated him.

The conspirators had motive to murder Strang; now they needed the opportunity. That opportunity would arrive when the *Michigan* returned to Beaver Island in June 1856. The captain, Charles H. McBlair, had heard stories about residents, like MacCulloch, who wanted to flee Strang's kingdom, and feared for their safety since they split with Strang's church. The *Michigan* would be the ideal getaway vehicle not just for the assassins, but also for the conspirators who faced possible reprisals from the Strangites.

The *Michigan* arrived on June 16, 1856. Several officers from the ship discussed matters on the island in MacCulloch's home. MacCulloch and others claimed that Strang and the Mormons were stealing their property, so Captain McBlair decided to invite Strang to the meeting to defend himself against the allegations.

It was the perfect chance for the assassins. When Strang approached, Bedford and Wentworth sneaked up behind him. They drew their pistols and fired at point-blank range. Bedford's bullet hit Strang in the head just above his left ear, and Wentworth's tore through the king's back and lodged in his spine.

Strang fell to the ground. Wounded, he looked up at his assassins. Wentworth had started toward the *Michigan*, but came back when he realized that the king wasn't dead. He stood over Strang and fired a third shot, which struck Strang in the right cheek, and then sprinted to the ship.

The third bullet did not satisfy Bedford, who proceeded to batter Strang with the butt of his pistol. Then Bedford raced to the *Michigan* and requested asylum. According to some eyewitnesses, the entire attack took place in view of several marines who watched it from the deck of the *Michigan* but did nothing.

Horrified Mormons hurried to their badly wounded king and took him to a nearby house, where Dr. James McClelland, the *Michigan*'s doctor, examined him. The first bullet severed an artery, which one Mormon plugged with his finger to staunch the bleeding. McClelland believed that Strang's wounds were fatal, but the king recovered enough to ask for custody of the two assassins.

The Strangites demanded that Captain McBlair turn over the two villains, but McBlair believed that the men would not receive fair treatment on Beaver Island. The Mormons likewise feared that because of anti-Mormon sentiment, the two would get nothing but a hand-slap at Mackinac.

The Mormons were right. Bedford and Wentworth were taken to jail, but they received the royal treatment. Citizens stopped by the jail to offer congratulations and brought them gifts of tobacco and whiskey. They weren't even charged for their time in jail—a common custom at the time. Three days later, Bedford and Wentworth faced a justice of the peace. After a hearing that lasted only an hour, they were released, but charged $1.25 each in court costs.

By June 26, Strang was still alive and even appeared to be improving. His kingdom, however, was under siege. Another steamship, also named *Michigan*, stopped at Beaver to obtain wood. Aboard the *Michigan* was a posse that included Hezekiah D. Mac-Culloch, and as if to add insult to injury, Thomas Bedford and Alexander Wentworth. They arrested a few Mormons and brought them aboard the steamer. They threatened to take Strang aboard as well, but they caused such a ruckus that a crowd formed, so they retreated to the ship and left the island.

The Mormon leadership, fearing another assassination attempt, decided to take Strang back to Voree on board the next ship leaving Beaver Island. The king left his kingdom aboard the *Louisville* on June 28, 1856. He warned other Mormons about possible reprisals, and an exodus from Beaver Island began.

Strang's vision proved accurate. An invasion force assembled on a nearby island called St. Helena. The group's leader, Archibald Newton, claimed that over the past few years, Mormons from Beaver stole several things from him, including fishing supplies and two oxen. Newton visited Beaver, but did not find the oxen. He did, however, find what appeared to be their hides. Now he had the opportunity to exact some revenge.

Newton landed on Beaver with a force of sixty armed men. They rounded up the Strangites still there, told them to gather their belongings, and ordered them to leave the island. Newton's gang then looted stores, burned down houses, and destroyed the Mormon tabernacle. They used Strang's house and library as a shooting range. The mob did a thorough job of tearing down what remained of the Mormon world on Beaver Island.

After appearing to be on the road to recovery, Strang took a turn for the worse. He died in his parents' home in Voree on July 9, 1856, at the age of forty-three. Strang's church atrophied after his death. He did not appoint a successor, and his followers, one by one, left for other faiths. Just a handful of Strangites remain today.

Strang's killers were never convicted of his murder. Alexander Wentworth moved to Minnesota. Shortly after the Civil War broke out, he joined the Minnesota infantry. He fought valiantly and earned promotion to sergeant, but died of disease in 1863 at the age of thirty.

Thomas Bedford stayed on Beaver Island for a few years after the assassination. He stood accused of another murder and was apparently arrested, but managed to escape the jail on Mackinac Island. He skipped the state before the case could go to trial. In 1864, Bedford enlisted and fought for the Union army. He returned to Michigan following the war, settling near a small town south of Lansing, and lived there until he died in 1889 of kidney failure at the age of seventy-six.

Little remains of Strang's vision or his kingdom on Beaver Island. The print shop still exists; it houses the Beaver Island Historical Society and Museum. Like his church, however, Strang's house disappeared, a board at a time, as souvenir hunters took pieces of his palace until nothing was left.

# CHAPTER 3

# Wild, Wild West: The Lawless Frontier of Michigan's Upper Peninsula

Boot Hill, saloons, gunfights, and men who died with their boots on. These are images typically associated with the Wild West of the American frontier. In the late nineteenth century, the Upper Peninsula was Michigan's western frontier, and it was as wild as, if not wilder than, the Wild West.

As railroads opened up the north, lumberjacks and miners migrated to the Upper Peninsula in search of fortune. Lumberjacks set up temporary camps in the deep white pine forests. After-hours, they ventured into the nearest towns to spend their pay. Boom towns, offering saloons, brothels, and gambling dens, became the scenes of drunken excess and near lawlessness.

The wildest place in Michigan's "Wild West" was a town called Seney. With its twenty-one saloons and two major brothels, Seney had a soul, but it didn't have a conscience, earning it the nicknames "Sin Town," "The Toughest Town in Michigan," and "Helltown, USA." In the late nineteenth century, folks used to say that if someone asked for a ticket to hell, the clerk gave him a ticket to Seney.

Seney was located in a vast pine forest about eighty-five miles from Sault St. Marie. In the late 1800s, about fifteen logging camps worked the virgin pine forests of Schoolcraft County, and when the lumberjacks wanted to unwind, they went to Seney.

The population of Seney at its peak of prosperity was about three thousand, but in the spring, when the lumber companies issued paychecks, the population of the small town swelled to double its size.

Work in the lumber camps was difficult. The hours were long, the work was dangerous, and the men, mostly bachelors, lived in dorm-style bunkhouses. They worked hard and played even harder. When they ventured into town, they went straight for the saloons and the bordellos.

Seney's prostitutes, like their customers, worked long hours. Hookers serviced lumberjack "johns" anywhere they could—behind sheds, in stables, even in the open. Many of them made small fortunes and pocketed thousands.

The sale of whiskey was as lucrative, if not more so, than the sale of love. Twenty-one saloons serviced thirsty visitors twenty-four hours a day. Lubricated lumberjacks often settled scores on tavern floors. Fights between drunken lumberjacks occurred often, prompting a local doctor to remark that a person could find his clinic by following the trail of blood through the snow.

Seney's many diversions attracted a motley cast of characters right out of a comic book. "Protestant Bob" McGuire was known for his long thumbnails, which he used as knives during fistfights. Another character, "Snag Jaw" P. K. Small, amused others and earned free drinks by biting the heads off of small animals. He even downed a live mouse in exchange for a shot of whiskey.

"Stub Foot" O'Donnell and "Pump Handle" Joe ambushed people getting off the train. They grabbed an unsuspecting traveler's ankles, upending him, and stole the cash that fell out of his pockets. Then, they bolted to the nearest tavern to buy drinks.

"Silver Jack" Driscoll, while not the town's sheriff, kept unofficial law and order with his fists. Known throughout the north as a brawler, most knew to stay away from Driscoll. Although they began as opponents in a bar fight years earlier, Driscoll became the muscle for Seney's most infamous citizen, Dan Dunn.

Dan Dunn, one of the most notorious figures in Michigan in the latter half of the nineteenth century, had brick-red hair and a fiery temper. Unlike most of the characters around Seney, Dunn did not drink or gamble. But like the others, Dunn liked to fight, and he had a lot of practice. When the going got tough, though, Dan Dunn got going; he would jack-rabbit when losing a brawl.

In the 1870s, Dunn worked at a place called Camp 16, a small lumberjack colony in the middle of Michigan's Lower Peninsula. The spot would later be called Edenville, but it would be anything but paradise for Dan Dunn. While at a nearby saloon, he picked a fight with Silver Jack Driscoll. Driscoll drubbed Dunn until the desperate and battered lumberjack grabbed a knife. Seeing the blade, Driscoll stepped back and Dunn darted from the saloon. The two would later make peace, and Driscoll would take a job at Dunn's Seney saloon.

After his scrap with Driscoll at Edenville, Dunn drifted north to Roscommon, where he hung up his lumberjack's axe and went to work as a bartender in a saloon and brothel. He saved his money and in 1878 opened his own bawdy house called Dunn's Bull Pen. The bulls migrated from the lumber camps to Dunn's pen to spend their hard-earned cash on female companionship. Dunn's red-light business was so profitable that he opened two franchises in other small towns nearby.

But it didn't take long for Dunn to find trouble again. While he was drinking at a bar with a friend named Jack Hayes, a fight broke out and shots were fired. An innocent patron was struck in the foot by a wayward bullet.

Two constables were dispatched to arrest the raucous men, who they found at the American House saloon. Hayes and Dunn attacked the constables. In the ensuing fight, one of the constables shot Hayes in the chest, killing him instantly. And once again, Dunn bolted. The constables managed to collar Dunn later that night. The feisty troublemaker did a short stint in jail and paid a fine.

By 1881, Dunn's business had begun to dry up; stiff competition and crooked sheriffs made it difficult to thrive. So, Dunn decided to relocate to Michigan's new frontier—the Wild West of the Upper Peninsula. By this time, railroads had opened up the UP, and lumberjacks drifted north to the virgin pine forests. Huge profits awaited anyone who could provide the two sirens that lured lumberjacks to town: booze and women.

Dunn spied an ideal location in Seney. He hired a man to burn down his bar in Roscommon, borrowed a sum of money from a druggist, and headed north for the tiny settlement.

If Seney became Michigan's Sin City, Dan Dunn played a large role in its development. He operated one of the town's twenty-one saloons and one of the two major brothels. He made a small fortune selling whiskey and women, but by this time, he had pushed aside his own use of the bottle and gambling. He married a local woman and became a major player in the politics of Schoolcraft County. In 1888, Dunn was instrumental in the election of county sheriff Dennis Heffron, who did his part to keep his patron out of jail.

Dunn's tin star was just a decoration. He made his own problems disappear before they caused him legal trouble. Not long after Dunn settled in Seney, the arsonist that he hired to incinerate his place in Roscommon came to Seney to squeeze him for hush money. Dunn lured the man to a remote property with the promise of a job clearing pine and then shot him in the back. Two lumberjacks who followed the pair from Seney witnessed the scene and watched as Dunn buried his victim in a shallow grave. Fearing Dunn, they left the vicinity only to return later to tell the tale.

The druggist who lent Dunn seed money also came to Seney to collect. Dunn told the druggist about a parcel of land he'd bought with the money. The land contained a rich deposit of iron ore, Dunn told the unsuspecting man. He led the druggist to the same property where he had murdered the arsonist. He shot the druggist in the head and buried the body. This murder remained unsolved until eyewitnesses later helped authorities locate the bodies.

But there was one problem that even Dunn couldn't solve: his competition in the lucrative trade of vice in Seney—the six Harcourt brothers. The Harcourt brothers ran a saloon and Seney's other major bordello. Like Dunn, their power and political influence grew with their fortune. And they didn't like Dunn any more than he liked them. Just a few years after the Earp brothers tangled with the Cowboys at the OK Corral in Tombstone, Arizona, the Dunn-Harcourt feud boiled over in Dunn's saloon.

The conflict began years earlier as a rivalry in Roscommon, but when the Harcourts and later Dunn relocated to Helltown, the rivalry escalated into a full-fledged feud. Dunn hired his old foe Silver Jack Driscoll as a bouncer. He planned to use Driscoll as a weapon to wage war against the Harcourts, but during a card game that turned contentious, Luke Harcourt chastised Driscoll for being Dunn's tool. Driscoll, unaware of Dunn's plan, confronted his boss. Silver Jack apparently didn't like Dunn's response, because he quit his bartending job at Dunn's saloon. Disgusted, Dan Dunn threatened to shoot the next Harcourt he saw.

The next Harcourt he saw was twenty-year-old Steve Harcourt, who brazenly waltzed into Dunn's saloon on June 25, 1891, and ordered a round of drinks for Dunn's patrons. For Dan Dunn, who considered himself the main man in Seney, this show of arrogance was just too much to take. He refused to serve the young Harcourt, and they began to argue and taunt each other. After a few minutes, their verbal sparring turned physical. Accounts vary as to who brandished a bottle first, but most agree that Dunn grabbed one and smashed Steve Harcourt on the head.

Then the shooting started. Like so many Wild West shootouts, the facts have become blurred by the various accounts told by inebriated bar patrons. Some say that Harcourt fired first, sending two shots at Dan Dunn. The first of the two hit Dunn in the hand, while the second bounced off the bar and struck the painting of famous boxer John L. Sullivan hanging on the wall behind Dunn.

Others say that Dunn fired first. In this version of the shooting, Dunn grabbed a pistol from the bar and shot Harcourt in the jaw. Harcourt stumbled and reached into his pocket for his pistol. He fired at Dunn, but he missed, his bullet grazing the top of the bar and striking the painting behind it.

Regardless of who fired the first shot, Dan Dunn's second bullet ended the argument. The slug hit Harcourt in the midsection. Dazed, Harcourt wobbled through the door and collapsed on the boardwalk outside the saloon. He died a few days later and was buried in Seney's Boot Hill Cemetery.

Dunn was arrested for manslaughter in nearby Manistique, but the judge presiding over the preliminary hearing found that Dunn had acted out of self-defense and discharged him. The Harcourts were livid and threatened to get even.

Terrified, Dunn fled Seney. An arrest warrant was issued for three of the Harcourt brothers, and Sheriff Heffron traveled to Helltown to arrest them. They agreed to face a judge, so Heffron and the Harcourt brothers boarded a train en route to Manistique.

At the time, Trout Lake was a major hub for the Upper Peninsula's railway traffic. Commuters with a layover often ambled over to Jack Nevens's tavern for a quick one. So when the train stopped at Trout Lake, a few of the passengers, including Heffron and the Harcourts, wandered over to the saloon for a drink while they waited for the connecting train to Manistique. When the Harcourts walked into the tavern, they recognized a familiar figure standing at the bar—Dan Dunn.

Dunn noticed Jim Harcourt out of the corner of his eye. He reached for his pistol and began to turn, but Harcourt was quicker, drawing his .32 and shooting Dunn three times. He only needed one; the first shot passed through Dunn's heart. Dunn crumpled to the floor, dead. According to some accounts, Jim Harcourt then stood over Dunn's body and fired two more bullets at Dunn's head. He missed, both bullets striking the floor. After the shooting, Jim handed the empty gun to Sheriff Heffron, who promptly arrested him and turned him over to the Chippewa County authorities.

A few months after murdering Seney's most infamous citizen, Jim Harcourt faced a jury in Sault St. Marie. Emotions ran high and just about everyone had an opinion about Harcourt's fate. Some believed that the assassin must pay dearly for shooting a man in the back, while others argued that Harcourt deserved an award for ridding the people of the "Northern Peninsula Terror."

Harcourt pleaded not guilty and maintained that he killed Dan Dunn in self-defense. The jury did not agree and sent Jim Harcourt to prison for seven-and-a-half years. But Jim had friends with powerful connections, and a friend-of-a-friend swayed Gov. John T. Rich to pardon him after three years. Jim Harcourt returned to a hero's welcome in Seney and began life as a public servant, first as town supervisor, then as deputy sheriff, and finally, as the conservation officer for Schoolcraft County. But by the time of Harcourt's return, Seney didn't have much of a public left to serve. The town had withered to a shadow of its former self.

Like many Upper Peninsula boomtowns, Seney's lifeblood were the lumberjacks who in turn depended on white pine. With the area deforested, the lumberjacks migrated north, and Michigan's Sin City died. Today, Seney is a small dot along highway M28, but the area is still a pretty wild place; just outside of town is the Seney National Wildlife Refuge.

While Dan Dunn and the Harcourt brothers sold sin to north woods lumberjacks, the good townspeople of Fayette did everything they could to keep sin out of their area and took measures to keep the riffraff in the forests. Their garden did have a few snakes, though. One of them was Jim Summers.

Michigan's Upper Peninsula was rich in iron ore as well as white pine, and at about the time the Civil War began, an agent of Jackson Iron Company named Fayette Brown found the ideal spot to build smelting furnaces. The tip of the Garden Peninsula—a peninsula shaped like a downward-pointed thumb jutting out into Lake

Michigan—had everything the company needed to begin a large-scale operation: a deep harbor for ships used to ferry the iron to Chicago at the base of Lake Michigan, limestone bluffs for building structures, and pine forests for charcoal.

So the town of Fayette was born in 1867. Unlike Seney sixty miles to the northeast, Fayette was a company town. Jackson Iron owned the land, which included about sixteen thousand acres of pine forests, the smelters, and the buildings. But people didn't mind. Work was fairly steady and the company paid high wages in gold. Fayette experienced a boom when its pig iron production took off in the 1870s and 1880s.

At its peak, the town's population—about five hundred—was just a fraction of Seney's, but it did have everything needed to make frontier life comfortable, including a post office, a hotel, and even an opera house. But it did not have a saloon.

In the 1870s, the state of Michigan began an early experiment with prohibition. In an attempt to follow the law, the company declared Fayette a dry town, and they banned alcohol on company property. They also outlawed prostitution. Jackson Iron wanted to keep its workers from vice, but it didn't quite succeed.

Ships with saloons docked off Fayette, and just outside the town limits, a few shady characters provided what Fayette merchants couldn't. One of them, Alph Berlanquette, ran a tavern called The Hole in the Ground

It was a profitable venture. Supposedly, Berlanquette amassed a fortune in gold coins spent by thirsty company employees and buried them somewhere on the property. For years, treasure hunters have dimpled the landscape in their search for Berlanquette's stash, despite rumors that someone found the cache in the early 1900s.

The Garden Peninsula also had a pimp—a mysterious character named Jim Summers. No two sources tell his story in the exact same way, but they all agree on one point: Jim Summers was a vile character. The *Crystal Falls Diamond Drill* described him as "one of the most disreputable and widely-known toughs in the Upper Peninsula."

Before he dropped anchor on the Garden Peninsula, Summers drifted from one lumberjack boomtown to another, migrating north from the Lower Peninsula and acquiring a reputation as a mean drunk, a brawler, and a sharpshooter with a quick temper. Like other nineteenth-century hooligans, he found his way to Seney, but the locals did not care for the troublemaking Summers and threw the gambler out of town.

In the early 1880s, Summers landed at The Hole in the Wall, where he drank with a group of ruffians who came to be known as the Summers Gang. Some say that Summers and his crew took over The Hole in the Ground and turned it into a bordello; others say that he built his place adjacent to the tavern. Either way, Summers opened a house of joy a short hike from Fayette.

For the women of Summers's brothel, the Garden Peninsula was far from a paradise. To keep his employees from leaving, Summers built a high fence around the bordello, virtually enslaving his prostitutes. People began to call it "the Stockade."

Business boomed as company men made the walk from Fayette to visit the Stockade's prostitutes. Then an incident occurred that brought down the Stockade fences for good. A pretty young woman arrived from Milwaukee and asked where she could find Jim Summers. Summers had hired her, she said, to take care of his ill wife.

This story raised a few eyebrows, because Summers wasn't married. Apparently, Summers had used the caretaker gambit to lure the woman into his Stockade. A few days later, she turned up bruised and beaten, lying next to the train tracks leading into town. The terrified woman pleaded for protection, but Summers showed up in a wagon and the local sheriff, perhaps afraid of Summers, turned her over to the pimp.

The people of Fayette had seen enough. It was now clear that Summers was holding women against their will. Prostitution was one thing, but they refused to turn a blind eye to kidnapping and slavery. So they formed a posse and stormed Summers's brothel. The enraged mob beat him and left him for dead on the beach of Bay de Noc. Then they ransacked the brothel and torched it.

Somehow, Summers survived. During the night, he regained consciousness and fled the area, some say in a rowboat. He was done in Fayette, but he was far from done causing trouble in the Upper Peninsula.

A few years later, Summers became entangled in a homesteaders' war, possibly as a hired gun fighting for the settlers. A group of squatters who settled the Paint River Valley feuded with the Metropolitan Lumber Company. The company claimed to have the right to fell the pine in the area, but the settlers didn't want to leave. They sabotaged company operations by pouring hot ash over roads to prevent lumber shipments. They shot company horses and drilled iron railroad spikes into trees to destroy company saws.

In the middle of the fight was Jim Summers, who went to work against the company with his Winchester. He allegedly intimidated the company's foreman by parting his hair with a bullet. When a local sheriff arrived to arrest Summers, the two exchanged lead before the sheriff fled.

The undoing of Jim Summers wouldn't be an angry posse or a quick-draw sheriff—it would be his temper. Like Dan Dunn's murder of Steve Harcourt, there are differing versions as to what exactly happened inside Kate Harrington's saloon in December 1891. Some say a local named Jerry Mahoney poked fun at the gunslinger. If Mahoney didn't shut up, Summers threatened, he would shut his mouth for him . . . with his rifle. Mahoney kept at it, and good to his word, Summers shot him in the face.

In a more realistic version, Summers, angry that the bartender would not lend him $10, began shooting wildly around the bar, one of his slugs hitting Mahoney in the face. The bullet struck Mahoney below the ear and tore through his jaw, removing a chunk of his tongue.

Summers hid out in the woods for a while as the local authorities searched for him. "His capture and incarceration," the *Diamond Drill* noted, "will rid the Upper Peninsula of a despicable character only equaled in wickedness by the deceased Dan Dunn, who met his merited fate 'with his boots on' several months ago." They never did catch Jim Summers. After living in the woods for several weeks, he left the Upper Peninsula and disappeared.

So did the town that tried to end Jim Summers's reign of terror in the UP. Fayette died when the area's timber ran out. Without charcoal, the smelters could not function, and the entire operation folded. Today, it is a state park where visitors stroll down dirt roads shaded by oak trees and wander through the skeletons of company buildings and homes decked out in the fashion of their heyday.

With thousands of acres of national forest, Michigan's Upper Peninsula is still wild, but characters like Dan Dunn and Jim Summers, who put the "wild" in the UP's Wild West, are long gone.

# CHAPTER 4

# The Subtle and Daring Poison Plot of Arthur Waite

In March 1916, the U.S. Army chased Pancho Villa into Mexico, and the Imperial German Army tangled with British and French forces at Verdun. But it was the murder of millionaire druggist John E. Peck that dominated headlines in Grand Rapids, Michigan, and New York City. The poison plot of Peck's son-in-law, Dr. Arthur Waite, was so shocking that it briefly pushed the Mexican bandit and trench warfare to the margins.

While the armies of Europe battled in the trenches, Dr. Arthur Waite declared war on his in-laws with an arsenal of dangerous germs and poisons. He would have gotten away with it, and kept murdering, if it were not for a mysterious telegram sent to Peck's son, Percy, by an armchair detective in New York.

Percy Peck was still mourning the unexpected loss of his mother when his father died less than two months later on March 11, 1916.

John E. Peck, the seventy-two-year-old pharmacist and self-made millionaire from Grand Rapids, enjoyed perfect health until he went to visit his daughter and her husband in New York City. But he became severely ill and passed away in his sleep in their Manhattan apartment. Peck's body was on a train headed to Grand Rapids for the funeral, and from there, to Detroit for cremation.

While he waited for the arrival of his father's body, Percy Peck received an alarming telegram from New York:

SUSPICION AROUSED STOP

DEMAND AUTOPSY STOP

KEEP TELEGRAM SECRET STOP

SIGNED K. ADAMS

Who was K. Adams? Percy Peck had never heard of him or her. Suspicion aroused? Demand autopsy? The language of the telegram hinted that John Peck might have been the victim of foul play.

K. Adams's cryptic message led to an investigation that uncovered what the *Grand Rapids Herald* of March 23, 1916, called "one of the subtlest, and at the same time, most daring poison plots that the criminal history of the country has known." The motive for the plot was John Peck's seven-figure fortune, which he began accumulating when he moved from New York to Grand Rapids in the 1860s.

Grand Rapids, a quiet, subdued city in the western part of Michigan, was just what the doctor ordered for John Peck and his new bride, Hannah. The son of an affluent surgeon and drug manufacturer from upstate New York, Peck served in the Union army during the Civil War. When the war ended, John decided to join his older brother Thomas, who had established a pharmaceutical business in Grand Rapids. The sleepy frontier town must have seemed quiet when compared to the battlefields back east, but it wouldn't stay quiet for long.

When John and Hannah Peck arrived in Grand Rapids, the city was on the verge of a population explosion. Westward expansion created a need for timber, causing lumber camps to appear all over

Michigan. Grand Rapids became a lumber trade depot and eventually evolved into the furniture capital of the United States.

Business thrived. John E. Peck amassed a fortune making and selling drugs and various sundries to the citizens of the boomtown. Peck's Drugs stood at the corner of Monroe and Division Avenues—one of the busiest intersections in the city. A smart businessman, Peck invested his profits wisely and his nest egg grew. He later became the president of several banks and a major stockholder in local furniture companies. As John Peck's fortune grew, so too did his family with the birth of a son, Percy, and a daughter, Clara Louise.

The Pecks lived in a Victorian mansion on the eastern edge of the city, on top of a hill that sloped gently downward to the Grand River. Percy and Clara Louise grew up with the children of lumber barons, bankers, and other prominent citizens. Like her high-society chums, Clara traveled east for a formal education. She went to a finishing school in Washington, D.C., and then went to Columbia University. Intelligent and gentle in demeanor, Clara dedicated much of her time after college to charity work at a local rehabilitation clinic for the physically disabled.

The Waites lived a short distance from the Pecks, but their lives couldn't have been more distant from the affluent lifestyle enjoyed by the wealthy druggist's family. Warren Waite supported his wife, Jennie, and three children as a fruit and vegetable wholesaler. They lived in a modest, two-story dwelling. One of the Waite boys, Arthur, would become one of the state's most infamous characters.

Arthur Warren Waite was born in 1886. He grew up around Michigan Avenue and attended Grand Rapids Central High School. By the time he graduated in 1905, he had developed a persona that women would find irresistible. Tall and athletic, Waite played baseball and football in school. Off the field, he participated in several school activities, including the high school literary society.

But young Arthur Waite also had a sinister side. He later said that as a child, he had tortured and killed animals, and he began at an early age to steal things and defraud people. He pilfered money from his job as a newsboy, and as a high school student, he climbed a fire escape to steal a test off of a teacher's desk.

After high school, Waite attended the University of Michigan, where he studied dentistry. He had a crafty intelligence, but he also continued to steal things. When he got behind in classes, he stole another student's work and submitted it as his own. He also swiped $100 from a friend's trunk. Arthur was caught both times, but was allowed to remain in school and managed to graduate.

Waite also graduated to larger, more complex deceptions. After college, he traveled to Scotland to attend medical school at the University of Scotland, where he learned dental surgery. Waite doctored his University of Michigan diploma to appear that he had earned an advanced degree, so he could then complete a two-year program in only six months.

From Scotland, Dr. Waite went to Cape Town, South Africa, where he worked for Wellman and Bridgman Dental Company. During his time in Africa, he amassed some money and sent $7,000 to his family in Grand Rapids—some of it stolen. Eventually, Waite was caught, red-handed, stealing from his employer. The company didn't renew his contract, so when World War I began, Waite left Cape Town and returned to Grand Rapids with $25,000 in bank checks, a colorful past, and a new South African accent.

While still in South Africa, Waite began corresponding with a young socialite he met in Grand Rapids named Clara Louise Peck. She would become the victim of Waite's biggest, most grandiose deception.

At some point during their youth, their worlds had collided: the dashing Arthur Waite and the pharmacy heiress. The two likely knew each other briefly as children, but at some point, Waite set his sights on the Michigan debutante and her family's fortune.

When Waite returned from Africa, he visited Clara and her family. Tall, handsome, and an accomplished tennis player, Waite's charm was irresistible. He came with a travelogue of stories about his adventures. With an elongated "a"—a brogue he acquired in Africa—Waite told exciting stories about practicing dentistry in

South Africa, about two sizable farms he purchased in East Africa, and about life on the Dark Continent. He won over Clara's mother, Hannah Peck, who considered him a prize for her only daughter. After a while, Clara fell for Arthur Waite.

Likewise, Waite had found his soul mate, or at least that is how it appeared to the Peck family. Waite played the role of love-struck suitor well, but he later admitted that he never loved Clara. He did, however, love her family's considerable fortune. With his eyes on the Peck money, Waite worked his charms.

They began a courtship that ended a year later in September 1915 with a wedding at the Fountain Street Baptist Church, a high-society affair that captured the headlines of local newspapers. Clara didn't know it when she ambled down the aisle to meet her Prince Charming, but her family's name would soon dominate the head-lines for weeks to come.

The ink on their marriage certificate wasn't even dry when Waite hatched a plan to steal the Peck fortune. The happy couple moved into an apartment at the Coliseum, one of the most expensive resi-dences in New York City, where they lived on a $300-a-month allowance from John Peck. Waite told family and friends that he performed surgeries at local hospitals. He even took Clara to sev-eral New York hospitals, where he told her he performed oral sur-geries. He would go inside and emerge twenty minutes later, having completed his work.

But it was all just a front. Behind the façade of a hard-working doctor, Waite lived the life of a millionaire playboy. He dined with young ladies, attended the theater, and played tennis. He also acquired samples of dangerous bacilli.

Waite read books about deadly poisons and bacteria. Posing as a doctor studying bacteria, he amassed a collection of dangerous germs. His collection eventually contained pneumonia, tuberculo-sis, diphtheria, typhoid, and others that he planned to use on his in-laws. With Hannah and John out of the way, his wife Clara would inherit John's considerable wealth, and Waite could live in comfort for the rest of his life.

His first target was his father-in-law's sister, Catherine Peck. Wealthy Aunt Catherine lived in a posh apartment in New York City. Like the other Pecks, she fell for Waite's façade as a debonair gentleman suitor. When Waite asked Aunt Catherine for money, she never denied him. She even gave him the diamond for Clara's engagement ring.

In a devious twist, Waite tried to make Aunt Catherine his first victim, perhaps believing that Clara would inherit a portion of her aunt's fortune. Waite read about arsenic in flypaper, so he burned a few sheets and mixed the residue into her food, but it didn't work.

Next, he spiked her food with doses of anthrax, typhoid, tuberculosis, and other deadly germs. Aunt Catherine still didn't get sick, so Waite searched for more deadly strains. He even ground up glass and mixed it with her favorite marmalade. Waite tried something new almost every day, but still, Aunt Catherine did not succumb.

His attempts on his wealthy patroness came to an end when John and Hannah Peck visited the couple in January 1916. Waite immediately turned his attention to his mother-in-law. "I had everything ready for her before she arrived," Waite later admitted. "Everything" consisted of influenza, pneumonia, streptococcus, and typhoid, which he mixed into the food of the first meal she ate. Waite slipped into the dining room ahead of the others with his test tubes and dumped their contents into Hannah's soup.

Unlike her sister-in-law, Hannah became sick. Waite played the role of concerned son-in-law. When Hannah got the chills, he brought her a foot warmer. He even had fresh flowers delivered every day. As his mother-in-law's condition worsened, he stayed by her side. She died less than a week after she arrived of what was presumed to be kidney disease.

Clara and her father John were crushed by the sudden, unexpected death of the Peck matriarch. They were also surprised when Waite said Hannah had told him she wanted to be cremated. Clara was slightly suspicious about her mother's death and wanted an autopsy, but John Peck said such a thing went against his wife's wishes. So after a funeral in Grand Rapids, Waite accompanied the body to a crematorium in Detroit. Hannah's ashes were brought back to Grand Rapids and buried at the Oak Hill Cemetery.

The bereaved John Peck returned to Grand Rapids, but the house was empty and memories loomed around every corner. Lonely and depressed, he traveled east to New York to visit family. In early March 1916, he was once again in the Waite residence at the Coliseum Apartments.

Waite immediately commenced attempts to murder John Peck. At first, he tried the same strategy that worked so effectively with Hannah. He spiked his father-in-law's food with pneumonia, typhoid, and tuberculosis. John was strong and in excellent health, and to Waite's dismay, he didn't become sick.

"Then I tried to make him sick by giving him big doses of calomel," Waite later said. "I gave him half a bottle at a time in his food," Waite admitted, along with a steady diet of more germs. Still, John appeared unfazed by this attack on his system.

Waite's attempts became bolder and more creative. "I gave him pneumonia germs," Waite said, "and took him riding in the rain. I wet the sheets of his bed at night to give him a cold." Still, the scheme didn't work.

The next day, Waite read a news item about soldiers gassed with chlorine, so he decided to try a chemical weapon on his father-in-law. Waite mixed chlorate of potash with hydrochloric acid and released the homemade chlorine gas in Peck's room. Even this didn't work.

So Waite tried something less creative. He purchased ninety grains of arsenic from a local pharmacy. He dosed everything Peck ate or drank—hot milk, soup, oatmeal, pudding—until Peck had ingested the entire ninety grains. When Arthur poisoned his father-in-law's tea, Clara noticed peculiar bits floating in the mug. The substance eventually dissolved and changed the tea's color. It was suspicious, but Waite dispelled her fears when he told her that he was giving her father medicine in his tea.

Finally, on March 11, 1916, John became deathly ill after a dinner of oysters. Clara made him some eggnog, but she had to run an errand, so Waite agreed to give it to John. When Clara returned two hours later, John was so sick that he couldn't keep down the eggnog. Clara later said that she saw the same peculiar substance floating in the eggnog as she saw in his tea.

That night, the seemingly concerned son-in-law placed a couch outside of Peck's room to keep a vigil. When he heard his father-in-law groan, Waite soaked a rag in chloroform and pressed it over Peck's face. Waite later explained that the chloroform was to ease John's pain, but the real reason may have been to stifle the sick man's groans so Clara didn't hear them. If she heard her father moan, Clara may have called a real doctor, who could have exposed her husband's poison plot.

Sometime early in the morning of March 12, John Peck died at the age of seventy-two. His fortune passed in equal shares to Percy and Clara. With the Pecks now out of his way, the smooth-talking Arthur Waite attempted to pressure Clara into willing her entire fortune to him in case she died unexpectedly.

Waite's diabolical plan was working perfectly. All he needed to do now was to get rid of the evidence. Waite signed Peck's death certificate and sent the body to a Manhattan mortuary for embalming. He then tried to convince Clara that her father should be cremated in Detroit after the family service in Grand Rapids.

Waite was getting away with murder, but he was about to become trapped by a secret he kept from his wife. Every afternoon for several months, he visited Room 1105 at the Plaza Hotel for a rendezvous with a cabaret singer named Margaret Horton.

Margaret, the twenty-four-year-old wife of an electrical engineer named Harry Mack Horton, came to New York to pursue a career as a singer. She first met Waite at the Academy of Music where she was performing. Waite became infatuated with the beautiful contralto and introduced himself. Horton was immediately impressed with the multitalented doctor, who could speak French, play the piano, and talk about theater and opera. The two became good friends. Later, they both attended a local language school where they spent a few hours a day together.

Waite persuaded the young singer to rent an apartment with him at the Plaza Hotel under the name of Dr. and Mrs. A. M. Walters. In their "studio," they conversed in French and read scenes from *Romeo and Juliet*. Horton later described her relationship with Waite as "platonic," but they spent every afternoon together and Waite even gave her a diamond ring. Margaret's older husband, Harry, later said that he knew of Margaret's relationship with Waite but considered it harmless. The friendship, however, would doom Waite, who didn't know that his Juliet would cause his murder plot to unravel.

While lunching with Margaret at the Plaza on February 22, 1916, Waite bumped into an acquaintance named Elizabeth Hardwick, a schoolteacher and the niece of longtime Peck family friend Dr. Cornell. Flustered, Waite introduced Margaret as a nurse. Elizabeth immediately became suspicious.

But when Elizabeth heard about John Peck's untimely death from her uncle, her suspicion grew into fear. Waite's marriage to Clara, followed by the deaths of Hannah and then John Peck in close succession, put the Peck fortune in Waite's hands—a powerful motive for murder. She raced to Central Station and sent a telegram to Grand Rapids. Unsure of her suspicions, she used a pseudonym—K. Adams.

While Waite and Clara were en route to Grand Rapids with John Peck's body, Percy Peck received K. Adams's telegram. Percy Peck took K. Adams's advice. When the train arrived, he took charge of his father's remains. He consulted two trusted allies: the family's pastor, Dr. Alfred Wishart, and longtime family physician, Dr. Perry Schurtz. Schurtz did the autopsy and removed key organs from John Peck's body, including the stomach, spleen, and lungs, which he sent to the University of Michigan's medical school.

While Percy eagerly awaited the toxicology results, Wishart and Schurtz traveled to New York and met with assistant district attorney Frank Mancuso and Dr. Otto Schultze, a New York medical examiner. They discussed the possibility of a plot to murder the Pecks. Mancuso sent a wire to Dr. Victor Vaughn at the University of Michigan to obtain the results of the toxicology tests done on John Peck's organs. Vaughn's response was shocking: Peck's organs contained enough arsenic to kill ten men.

At 4:00 A.M. on the morning of March 18, Mancuso and the two men from Grand Rapids searched the Waite apartment. They found some provocative evidence of a possible poison plot: In the library, they found a book about drugs, *Wood's Therapeutics and Pharmacology*, with the bookmark in the page that described the effects of arsenic on the human body. But they didn't have enough for an arrest; a book wouldn't do it.

Meanwhile, a nervous Arthur Waite boarded a train headed for New York while his grief-stricken wife stayed in Grand Rapids. As soon as Waite arrived in New York, he began an attempt to cover up his crimes. He knew that doctors would discover arsenic during the autopsy, and he needed a way to explain how the poison got there. So, he attempted to bribe the undertaker to say that he used arsenic when preserving the body.

Waite knew that in 1907, the state of New York banned the use of arsenic in embalming. The law resulted from a case in which a man accused of poisoning another man claimed that the presence of arsenic in the victim's lungs was the result of embalming, not poisoning. Waite didn't know that by 1916 doctors could determine if arsenic was ingested before or after death.

Waite also didn't know that detectives were trailing him. The detectives witnessed the acts of a guilty man on the run. When Waite stopped to make a call from a telephone inside a pharmacy, a detective stood in the next booth and eavesdropped. "Pack and get out at once," Waite said. The call was to a Mrs. A. M. Walters in Room 1105 at the Plaza Hotel.

As Waite tried to cover his trail, Mancuso and Drs. Schultze, Schurtz, and Wishart traveled to Grand Rapids to continue the investigation. On March 21, Schultze and Schurtz conducted a second post mortem on John Peck's remains. It was decided that a second examination was needed to eliminate the possibility that the arsenic found in Peck's organs was the result of the embalming fluid used in New York. They removed the brain and sent it to the University of Michigan's medical school. Once again, the toxicology test revealed a huge quantity of arsenic. This second autopsy sealed Waite's fate.

The next day, detectives arrived at the Waite apartment in New York to arrest Arthur for murder. They pounded on the door, but no one answered. Inside the apartment, they found Waite on the bed, unconscious. He had overdosed. Investigators rushed him to Bellevue Hospital, where he remained in a coma for two days before regaining consciousness.

When Waite became conscious, he denied murdering John Peck or ever purchasing poison. But Waite couldn't explain a signed druggist's receipt dated March 9, which proved he bought arsenic, so he changed his story. He said that Peck was depressed after his wife's death and wanted to commit suicide. According to Waite, Peck asked for his help, so he bought the arsenic at a local pharmacy and gave it to him in a sealed envelope.

But the pile of evidence was mounting against Waite. Detectives found a former maid who Waite paid $1,000 to say that John Peck wanted to commit suicide. And they found the Manhattan undertaker Waite attempted to bribe. The man led detectives to a sandbank on Long Island, where he hid the wad of banknotes that Waite gave him to say he used arsenic when embalming John Peck's body.

Faced with the evidence, Waite changed his story again. He confessed to everything but added a bizarre accomplice. "The man from Egypt" made him do it, he told astonished prosecutors. "I never saw him," Waite said. "But he has been with me always. He made me do evil."

Clara followed the news with horror as the truth about her husband began to emerge. In the newspapers, Waite's biography of deception and fraud grew with each new edition. More and more people came forward to expose Waite as a cheat and a philanderer.

On March 25, Clara broke her silence and issued a statement to the press. "When I was informed of the serious charges against my husband," she said, "I could not believe them. It seemed impossible that a man who had been so uniformly gentle and kind to me and apparently so loyal could be guilty of the crime with which he was charged."

"My faith began to be shaken," Clara explained, "when it was practically proved to me that Dr. Waite was living with another woman at the Plaza Hotel." Then came the details of the arsenic plot, and Clara could no longer stand by her man.

In April, Clara filed for divorce. In her divorce suit, she cited the murders and her husband's tryst with Margaret Horton, who insisted that her relationship with Waite was never intimate—they were just friends who met at the Plaza Hotel to study together in their studio.

Margaret and her husband Harry gave a detailed statement to prosecutors. Margaret knew nothing of Arthur's plot to murder the Pecks, and when the details of his crimes emerged, she began to suspect his motives. She believed that Waite intended to poison both her and her husband to obtain their money.

According to Margaret, Waite believed that the Hortons were well off. Waite had also wanted to give her medicine, which now looked like a prelude to murder. Prosecutors speculated that Waite's real motive for murdering Margaret, if indeed he planned to murder her, was to cover up his involvement with the pretty cabaret singer. They also speculated that Waite may have planned on running away with Horton after he finished off the Pecks.

Waite's body count would have included three others: Clara, Percy, and Aunt Catherine. According to Percy, after John Peck's funeral, Waite told him that Clara looked ill and would only live a few more months. Later that same day, Waite told Clara that he didn't think Percy had much time left. And he told both Percy and Clara that Aunt Catherine was near the end. These comments suggest that Waite planned to murder the entire Peck family to steal their fortune.

Waite ultimately did more than hint. The *New York Times* of April 3, 1916, carried the headline "Waite Now Admits Intent to Kill Wife." According to the article, Waite confessed to his lawyer that Clara was going to be his next victim. Waite also said that he never loved Clara, only her money. Adding insult to injury, he said that with his plain-Jane wife out of his way, he could marry a more attractive woman, possibly referring to Margaret Horton.

By the time the murder trial began in late May, Waite had abandoned the "man from Egypt" story. His life now depended on a bold defense strategy. If he told the graphic details of his crimes in a cool, detached tone and insisted he was sane, the jury would consider him a "moral imbecile" and send him to an institution. In a strange twist, the usual roles of the prosecutor and the defense were reversed. Waite's lawyers were going to try to emphasize the depravity of the defendant, while the prosecutors were going to show that he wasn't as disturbed as he appeared.

Waite began his testimony with a sketch of his early days. He colored himself as a juvenile criminal who stole anything he could. He pilfered from his family, friends, and later, employers. He also said that he tormented the family cat and drowned her kittens.

Waite proceeded to detail the various attempts he made to murder his in-laws. He described the various germs he dumped into John Peck's food and his attempt to gas his father-in-law with homemade chlorine gas. When he described the outrageously diabolical ways he tried to infect John with pneumonia, such as placing ice water in his boots, one juror broke out laughing. Waite, though, didn't break a smile as he described his cold-blooded murders.

Exactly what Waite actually did to the Pecks is clouded by his own admissions. Waite's defense strategy was to prove his own depravity; therefore, he may have embellished, although his motive in the crimes and the end result remained clear.

Margaret Horton destroyed Waite's insanity defense when she testified for the prosecution. The twenty-four-year-old walked up to the stand in a black dress, black hat, and veil, as if dressed for a funeral. The *New York Times* of May 25, 1916, remarked that when she raised her veil, "it could not be denied that she possessed her share of a certain appealing beauty."

She described the history of her relationship with Waite and explained how they came to share their "studio" apartment together at the Plaza Hotel. When asked about the nature of her relationship, Horton testified that it was purely platonic.

Horton also described the contents of a letter Waite wrote her from Bellevue Hospital. In the note, Waite said that he expected to spend some time in an asylum for his crimes, but would eventually be free. He also acknowledged the possibility that he could get "la chaise"—the chair—for his crimes and said that he would fight for his life out of his love for her. This letter, the prosecution argued, proved that Waite was attempting to feign insanity.

Margaret's testimony was devastating to Waite's defense. The jury convicted Waite of first-degree murder and the court sentenced him to die in the electric chair. Waite stood calmly when he heard the sentence. He thanked the court and said he only wished that he had two bodies to give for the two victims he murdered.

On May 24, 1917, war raged in Europe. Congress passed the Selective Service Act, giving President Woodrow Wilson the ability to conscript soldiers. But once again, these stories were pushed to the margins in Michigan and New York newspapers by the Waite case.

On that day, Waite went to "la chaise" in Sing Sing. He was a cool customer, even for his executioner. He kept his composure, smiled, and said nothing as he took his place on the hot seat. After the first jolt of 2,000 volts, a prison doctor detected a faint heartbeat. A second jolt of 2,000 volts ended the story of Dr. Arthur Warren Waite's "subtle" and "daring" poison plot.

# CHAPTER 5

# Dynamite Farmer:
# Andrew Kehoe and History's
# Deadliest School Day

The worst loss of life in a public school did not occur at Columbine High School or on the campus of Virginia Tech. The deadliest school day in U.S. history occurred at Bath Consolidated School in the tiny village of Bath, Michigan, a few miles northeast of Lansing. In 1927, a disgruntled former school board member destroyed an entire wing of Bath Consolidated School with high explosives. Andrew Kehoe's devious plan consumed the lives of forty-five people, mostly young children, and injured dozens of others.

On May 18, 1927, Kehoe executed a plan weeks if not months in the making. The first in a sequence of events that rocked the tiny

**49**

community began at about 8:45 A.M. Kehoe's neighbors heard popping sounds, like gunshots, coming from his farm. In a gesture that seemed to say "If I can't have it, nobody can," Kehoe detonated some high explosives on his property, setting the farm buildings on fire.

At about the time that neighbors noticed the Kehoe farm burning, a massive blast leveled half of Bath Consolidated School. At 8:45 A.M., just after the morning bell signaled the beginning of classes, a timer triggered the explosives that Kehoe had planted throughout the school's north wing. The explosion was so powerful that it shattered nearby windows and set trees on fire. Eyewitnesses inside the building described hearing a loud "crashing" sound.

The explosion destroyed the entire north wing, where the third through sixth grades were in session. The force of the blast slammed some kids against the walls and threw others through the windows. Many students were crushed in their desks and buried under tons of rubble when the ceiling collapsed and the walls crumbled.

Students in the undamaged south wing made their way through the fog of dust and plaster and got out of the building in any way they could. Bewildered teachers escorted confused and terrified students to safety. On the first floor, students leaped from windows, which were shattered by the blast.

Frantic townspeople raced to the building and began clawing through the debris. Eyewitness Monty Ellsworth arrived at the school to find a macabre scene. Children were pinned beneath the collapsed roof, "and some of them had arms sticking out, some had legs, and some just their heads sticking out," Ellsworth said in *The Bath School Disaster*, a book he authored about the tragedy. "They were unrecognizable because they were covered with dust, plaster, and blood."

Within minutes, dozens of people began the effort to remove children trapped in the rubble. The rescuers followed the muffled screams coming from under the piles of wreckage.

While flames consumed his farmhouse, Kehoe drove off to the Bath Consolidated School in a truck loaded with bits of rusty metal—old shovels, nails, and other metallic flotsam—and a pile of dynamite in the back seat.

Concerned neighbors who raced to the Kehoe farm after they heard explosions there came across Kehoe leaving in his Ford truck. "You are my friends, you better get out of here," he told them. "Go down to the school," Kehoe said, and then he drove off toward Bath. He cruised around the area for awhile before heading to the school.

About twenty minutes after the explosion, Kehoe arrived at the ruins of Bath Consolidated School. He parked his truck and motioned to Superintendent Emory Huyck, who walked over to the vehicle. While Huyck stood by the truck, his leg propped up on the truck's running board, Kehoe turned and fired a rifle into the pile of explosives sitting in the back seat.

This second explosion turned Kehoe's truck into a giant grenade as the rusty junk tore through anyone standing nearby. The blast killed Kehoe and Huyck and fatally wounded three others: the town's postmaster, an elderly resident, and an eight-year-old child who had just survived the school bombing.

One eyewitness, quoted in the *New York Times* of May 20, 1927, described the grisly scene: Under a "great cloud of black smoke" was "the tangled remains of a car. Part of a human body was caught in the steering wheel." A portion of a human torso landed in front a nearby house. The pocket contained Kehoe's driver's license and a bankbook in his name.

For the next two hours, the rescue effort continued. One by one, the broken bodies of children were removed from the rubble and placed on the school's lawn. Piercing screams from desperate parents signaled the discovery of another child's body. A few homes became makeshift hospitals for the wounded. City Hall became a temporary morgue.

Ghastly, pathetic scenes were enacted by townspeople at the site. One local man sat next to the bodies of his two sons for more than an hour, sobbing. Shocked mothers cradled the lifeless bodies of their children. The *Toledo Blade*'s coverage of the event contains a photograph of a student's Raggedy Ann doll under the headline "Raggedy Ann Survives, Little Mother Dies."

News of the Bath disaster spread quickly. Consumers Energy employees, working in the vicinity, raced to join the relief effort. Firefighters from local communities, employees from two construction companies in nearby Lansing, the Michigan State police, and Red Cross workers all arrived in Bath to help. Even Michigan governor Fred Green traveled to the town to work amid the ruins. The dozens of people on school grounds turned into hundreds.

Searching through the debris, police officers found a surprise: explosives connected by an intricate network of wiring. They followed the wiring to the undamaged part of the school, where they found more explosives wired to a battery and a clock. At 10:45 A.M., approximately two hours after the first blast that leveled the north wing, police decided it was too dangerous to continue working around an undetonated time bomb. The discovery of the explosives forced a temporary halt on the attempts to remove the children buried under the remains of the north wing.

By the time they were done, investigators had removed 504 pounds of unexploded material, including both dynamite and pyrotol, a high explosive used during World War I. After the war, the U.S. government sold surplus pyrotol to farmers, who typically used the material to excavate ditches or remove rocks and tree stumps.

The cache of high explosives, deposited under the floors of every room, indicated that Kehoe planned to dynamite the entire school. For some reason, the the dynamite in the south wing never detonated.

There are several theories as to why the south wing didn't explode. Perhaps Kehoe made an error when he wired the devices. Or the quake caused by the blast that leveled the north wing caused a disruption in the wiring that spared the south wing and prevented further loss of life. Or the batteries designed to give life to the deadly mechanism didn't contain enough juice to detonate all of the pyrotol and dynamite. Whatever its cause, the electrical failure saved the rest of the Bath student body.

With the explosives removed, the relief work continued. The search for missing children went through the afternoon and into the evening. Those with minor injuries returned home, while seriously injured victims were transported to Lansing hospitals. One boy, ironically, was transported to an area hospital in the town's hearse.

Investigators combed the ruins of Kehoe's farm. They had learned that on Monday evening, he picked up his wife Nellie in Lansing and brought her to their farm in Bath. She had been chronically ill for about a year and spent time in area hospitals receiving treatment. One of Nellie's sisters spoke with Kehoe on Tuesday, May 17. Kehoe told her that Nellie had gone to visit friends in Jackson and would be back on Thursday. But the friends in Jackson hadn't seen or heard from Nellie. Neither had anyone else since she left the Lansing hospital, and investigators feared that they would find Nellie in the incinerated farmhouse.

They smothered the flames with chemicals, but the fire still raged. When the blaze died down later, they searched the house and the other buildings on the property. They discovered the homemade devices Kehoe used to destroy the house, the farm's outbuildings, and two horses, but they did not find Nellie.

The next day, May 19, 1927, their search came to an end behind a shed on Kehoe's farm, where they found the charred remains of Nellie Kehoe in a cart along with burned pieces of silverware and a cashbox filled with singed fragments of banknotes. Her corpse was so disfigured that several people had walked by without noticing it. Nellie, it became evident, was Kehoe's first victim. Sometime between Monday, May 17, and Wednesday, May 19, Kehoe had murdered his wife, probably by bashing her in the head with a blunt object. He tied her body to the cart and, along with some personal valuables, set it on fire.

During one of the searches, they also found Kehoe's last statement to the world. He left a provocative message printed on a wooden plank that was wired to the fence: "Criminals are made, not born."

The handmade sign raised a disturbing question. What drove Andrew Kehoe to slay his wife, burn down his home, and bomb a school? With the dust settled, the search for answers began. Who was the man the *New York Times* and other papers called "the Michigan Maniac?" Who was the man who Monty Ellsworth described as "the world's worst demon"?

Kehoe was born and raised on a farm in the small community of Tecumseh, Michigan, in 1872. Kehoe's father Philip moved to Michigan from Maryland and prospered, eventually running a large spread. As a child, Kehoe loved to tinker with equipment and was enamored with the young science of electricity.

In 1890, Kehoe's mother Mary passed away after a lengthy illness. Phillip Kehoe remarried a teenager named Francis Wilder, who was younger than her new husband's eighteen-year-old son Andrew. The young bride and her older stepson did not get along well. So Andrew left home and traveled to East Lansing, where he attended Michigan State College and studied electrical engineering.

While in college, Kehoe met Ellen "Nellie" Price, the daughter of a prominent local family. Nellie's uncle, Lawrence Price, ran a plant that produced automobile parts, and he contributed funds that led to the construction of Lansing's Sparrow Hospital—one of the places that later treated the victims of Kehoe's plot.

Nellie and Andrew dated for a while, but the two eventually split and Andrew traveled west to Missouri, where he continued his education in electrical engineering. While in Missouri, he had an accident, possibly a fall. He suffered a serious head injury that left him in a coma for two weeks. He eventually recovered and worked for a while in Iowa before returning to Michigan. In 1905 he moved back home and began working his family's farm.

The relationship between Andrew and his stepmother did not improve. His father, who suffered from severe arthritis, depended on Francis for everything, and Andrew disliked her more than ever. But the two managed to coexist for a few years until an incident occurred in 1911.

Francis went into the kitchen to cook lunch. When she lit the pilot light on the stove, it exploded, saturating her with oil and starting a fire. Andrew attempted to help by throwing a bucket of water on her, but the water only fueled the flames, and she later died from her injuries. Neighbors speculated that someone, possibly Andrew, had sabotaged the stove, but no official investigation was conducted.

A few months after his stepmother's tragic death, forty-year-old Andrew Kehoe married his college girlfriend, Nellie Price. He had reignited his relationship with Nellie, and the pair made it official in May 1912. The newlyweds first settled in Tecumseh, where Kehoe continued to work his father's farm. Philip Kehoe died a few years later, and the Kehoes decided to relocate.

In 1919, the couple purchased a small farm in Bath from Nellie's family. It was familiar territory to Nellie, who grew up on the 80-acre parcel. Neighbors who knew the Kehoes before and after they moved to Bath described Andrew Kehoe as a highly intelligent man, an expert electrician who loved to tinker with machinery.

He was somewhat of a perfectionist and meticulous in his affairs. Although he worked on machinery often, Kehoe rarely showed up in public with even a grease stain on his clothes. His farm equipment was spotless, and he kept the farm's outbuildings so clean that Ellsworth later said that Kehoe's farm was cleaner than many of his neighbors' houses.

Kehoe's attention to detail, along with tendency to be argumentative, earned him a reputation as a difficult man. At euchre parties, he would often chide players who deviated from Hoyle's rules.

Neighbors and acquaintances also described Kehoe as a kind, but somewhat distant, Uncle Scrooge–like character, an intractable skinflint. When it came to money, Kehoe liked to have his way and sometimes divorced himself from those who did not agree. When Kehoe lived in Tecumseh, he purchased eight steers and drove them into a wet clover pasture. A few of the animals died from eating the damp clover, and Kehoe asked the seller to refund part of his payment. The seller refused, and Kehoe quit speaking to the man.

On another occasion, Kehoe threw a priest off of his Tecumseh farm. Devout Catholics, he and Nellie attended Mass until the parish assessed him $400 for the construction of a new church. When Kehoe refused to pay, a priest visited him, and Kehoe ordered the priest to leave his property at once. If the priest didn't leave, Kehoe threatened that he would help him.

He might have made good on the threat if the priest hadn't left of his own free will—Kehoe had a violent side. He shot one neighbor's dog for burying a bone under his fence, and he told another neighbor that he beat one of his horses so severely that it died.

Kehoe may have been cheap and sometimes violent, but he also had a generous side. He often did favors for people without payment. He fixed a boiler for a neighboring farmer, and according to Ellsworth, he let others use his telephone without charge.

But he blanched when people asked him to pay for something. School taxes continued to rise in Bath because of the construction of a new school in 1922. In Michigan at the time, school taxes were levied at a rate per thousand dollars of property value, and Kehoe was bothered by what he saw as an excessive tax burden on his sizable farm. He decided to do something about it and ran for the school board.

In 1924, he was elected and became the board's treasurer. Kehoe quickly earned a reputation for inflexibility and would move to end meetings when someone disagreed with him. He also began to feud with Superintendent Huyck, telling him during one meeting that he did not belong in board meetings. He even tried to keep Huyck from a summer vacation, but eventually sided with the rest of the board to give the superintendent a one-week break. Sometimes, he purposely delayed delivering the superintendent's paycheck.

Despite his best efforts, though, Kehoe failed to make the changes he felt necessary. So when the township clerk died, he saw an opportunity and was appointed interim clerk to complete the term. But his reputation preceded him and he didn't win election in the spring of 1926.

A few months later, in October 1926, foreclosure proceedings began on the Kehoe farm. For some reason, Kehoe had abruptly stopped making mortgage payments years earlier. Nellie's persistent illness and frequent hospital stints may have contributed to Kehoe's fiscal slide, but he pointed his finger at the school board. When he was served notice of the foreclosure, he remarked that a school tax kept him from paying off the mortgage to the Price estate.

Some sources cite these two events—the election loss and the foreclosure notice—as lighting a fuse in Kehoe's mind. Whatever unknown, malignant motive moved him, Kehoe began to plot the downfall of Bath Consolidated. While the public Andrew Kehoe attempted to make changes through official channels, the private Andrew Kehoe schemed, formulating a systematic plan of destruction that took months of preparation. The exact time when Kehoe hatched his plot remains unknown, but it may have been well over a year earlier.

According to the inquest that followed the bombing, Kehoe purchased 500 pounds of pyrotol in Jackson in October 1925 and continued to add to the stockpile. Over time, he amassed hundreds of pounds of high explosives, including Hercules dynamite. He used the explosives, neighbors believed, to remove rocks and tree stumps, which was a common practice at the time. Kehoe's frequent use of explosives prompted one neighbor to call him a "dynamite farmer."

But Kehoe apparently didn't acquire all of the explosives to use on his farm. He had decided to attack the people of Bath by targeting the school and its students. Kehoe began to plant the pyrotol and dynamite throughout the school sometime late in 1926.

That year, the school board hired Kehoe to do some work on the electrical wiring inside the building. Now with free and unsupervised access to the school, Kehoe began to deposit and rig the explosives that brought down half of Bath Consolidated.

There were signs that Kehoe was plotting something. On New Year's Eve of 1927, he detonated a quantity of pyrotol on his farm. The boom startled neighbors, who wondered what caused the midnight blast. He was testing a clock timer, Kehoe told neighbors. Six months later, he would employ similar mechanisms on the school.

Kehoe's conversations also contained subtle, ominous warnings. Ten days before the tragedy, when Kehoe gave a bus driver his paycheck, he told the man that it would most likely be the last one he received. On Monday, May 16, a teacher asked Kehoe if she could host a party on his property on Thursday, May 19. Kehoe consented, but told her not to wait until Thursday. For many of the children, Kehoe knew, Thursday would never come.

And for many, it didn't. Kehoe executed his plan on Wednesday, May 18. The tragedy created a boom heard for ten miles and felt throughout the United States. Headlines across the nation carried news about the "Michigan Maniac" and the village school he attacked.

On the Saturday and Sunday following the tragedy, as Bath residents buried their dead, a long procession of curious spectators flooded the tiny town. People came from all over Michigan to pay their respects or to catch a glimpse of the devastated structure. Estimates place the number of cars at over fifty thousand on Sunday alone, and the sheer volume of vehicles caused traffic backups for miles in all directions.

The coroner's inquest took place the week after the disaster. The inquest found Kehoe responsible for forty-four deaths: thirty-seven children ages seven through fourteen; Superintendent Huyck and two teachers; an elderly resident; the Bath postmaster; Nellie Kehoe; and Andrew Kehoe himself. A fourth-grader who died later brought the total to forty-five.

But what really was his motive? Most contemporary media accounts characterized Kehoe as a man obsessed with high taxes He blamed the school for his financial woes. "It is believed," an article in the *New York Times* of May 19, 1927, noted, "Kehoe's mad act was caused by his desire for revenge on the School Board." The claim was repeated in the next day's issue: Kehoe wanted to "wreak vengeance on this community for what he felt was the high tax imposed on him and other financial troubles."

Acquaintances interviewed at the inquest noted that the disgruntled farmer did speak against what he felt were exorbitantly high taxes. Kehoe said, "The taxes was so excessively high he didn't know what would become of us," one person noted. But Kehoe didn't seem atypically enraged over the issue. "He wasn't so very rabid about it," another acquaintance said.

And even though Kehoe stood in a financial hole, he probably wouldn't have lost his home to foreclosure; the Price estate was gentle about Kehoe's mortgage and would have allowed him to sell the farm to settle his debt. Still, after the bombing, many people speculated that in Kehoe's mind, the potential loss of his farm was linked with the existence of the school, so he decided to deprive his creditors by destroying both. Or maybe there was another cause— something broken in his mind, some faulty wiring in his brain.

Not according to public officials. "We find that the said Andrew P. Kehoe was sane at all times," the official inquest concluded.

Despite the findings of the inquest, the search for a way to comprehend Kehoe's rampage continued. One group labeled him as manic depressive. Others turned to other explanations. "What queer streak in his make-up made him plan with demonic cunning, the dynamiting of a school filled with small children?" a reporter for the *Toledo Blade* wrote in a May 23, 1927, article entitled "Killer's Skull to Be Studied." A portion of Kehoe's skull survived the blast, and a Michigan university requested the fragment for analysis.

It appeared that Kehoe was going to have his head examined for possible clues about his behavior. According to the *Blade* article, there was also some talk about the contours of Kehoe's cranium, and a few were convinced he "was a strange throw-back to the primitive day, who may have been bewildered by being forced to live under civilization's laws."

Bath was front-page news until Charles Lindbergh touched down on a Paris airfield—the first non-stop flight from New York to Paris. Lindbergh's transatlantic flight captivated the nation and dominated the headlines. The Bath bombing disappeared from the front pages and became a bloody footnote in U.S. history.

But the tragedy was not forgotten. Today, the spot where Andrew Kehoe attempted to destroy the legacy of Bath is a memorial park. A plaque on a large rock lists the names of Kehoe's victims.

A local museum also memorializes the tragedy by displaying items such as the American flag that flew over Bath Consolidated School the day that Kehoe leveled it.

Kehoe was buried in an unmarked grave in the pauper's section of a neighboring community's cemetery. Without a tombstone, his only epitaph is the sign that he left on his fence bearing the enigmatic message, "criminals are made, not born."

# CHAPTER 6

# Motor City Massacre and the End of the Purple Reign

On the afternoon of September 16, 1931, a resident of Collingwood Manor—a quiet apartment complex on Detroit's west side—heard strange, popping sounds coming from Apartment 211 on the floor above. She went to the stairwell and was almost knocked over by a man racing down the steps. She alerted Frank Holt, the building manager, who went upstairs to see what was causing the commotion. Holt knocked on the door. No one answered.

After a few seconds, he opened the door to find one of the bloodiest crime scenes in the city's history. So much blood had pooled on the floor that it began to soak through the floorboards and into the apartment below.

The Collingwood Manor Massacre, Detroit's version of the St. Valentine's Day Massacre, was the signature moment for the gang with a reputation as America's most ruthless outfit—the Purple Gang. It also led to the end of their reign over Prohibition-era Detroit.

No one knows the exact origin of the name Purple Gang. Some believe that a newspaper reporter coined the nickname during the height of the gang's power. Others believe that the name originated with an East Detroit shopkeeper who described the juvenile delinquents as rotten, or "purple." Regardless of the name's origin, the kids that grew up to rule Prohibition-era Detroit became known as the Purples.

The Purple Gang formed in an area of East Detroit around Hastings Street. This area, known as Paradise Valley, was populated by Eastern European immigrants, mostly working-class Jews who came to Detroit from New York.

East Detroit in the teens and twenties was a rough place. The infant auto industry and Henry Ford's assembly lines brought huge numbers of people to the new boomtown, but overcrowding and poverty led to a spike in crime.

The population boom also spawned other industries. Saloons appeared on every street corner and remained open at all hours to service all three shifts of workers. Brothels and gambling houses serviced other needs. Eventually, crime syndicates were organized to control the lucrative business of vice.

The Bernstein boys, who would one day lead the Purple Gang, grew up in this area—Detroit's "Little Jerusalem"—earning an education on the streets. Their father, Harry Bernstein, a Polish Jew who emigrated from Russia, moved from New York to Detroit in 1902 and opened a shoe repair shop on Gratiot Avenue. He and his wife tended the shop during the day and lived above it at night. Their family eventually grew to include seven children, three girls and four boys. The boys were Abe, Joe, Raymond, and Isadore.

Abe dropped out of school and later went to work in Detroit's underground casinos. While he learned to deal cards, his brothers went to the school of hard knocks, scrapping their way through life in Paradise Valley. Like their brother, they weren't interested in academics and wound up in the ungraded section of the Old Bishop School. In this wing, a trade school for problem children of all ages, the Bernstein brothers rubbed elbows with other troublemakers from the neighborhood. These toughs formed the core of the gang. They began with petty crimes, such as running craps games and extorting protection money from shop owners. The boys remained small-time crooks until 1918, when a law transformed them into one of America's leading crime syndicates.

In 1918, Prohibition became law in the Great Lakes State and Michigan dried out. Detroit was the first major U.S. city to undergo the "Noble Experiment" of prohibition, but the demand for liquor actually increased. When Prohibition began in Michigan, Detroit had fifteen hundred licensed taverns and eight hundred unlicensed taverns, called blind pigs. By 1925, seven years into the state's prohibition era, the number of blind pigs had exploded. In Detroit alone, an estimated twenty thousand illegal "gin joints" serviced the needs of thirsty customers.

Massive profits awaited anyone who could quench America's thirst for booze, and organized crime took over the lucrative trade in alcohol. Fortunes were made almost overnight as rumrunners ferried illegal spirits across the borders into the United States.

Detroit sat at the crossroads of this black-market trade. The geography of the area transformed the Motor City into a bootlegger's heaven. The narrow Detroit and St. Clair Rivers separate Michigan from Canada—a short distance for smugglers, who brought liquor across on boats. When the rivers froze over in the winter, Model Ts carried cases of Canadian whiskey across the ice.

The traffic was heavy; during the mid-1920s, three-quarters of all illegal booze brought into the United States traveled through

Detroit and the "Windsor Funnel." This vast criminal enterprise of gambling, prostitution, drugs, and now alcohol offered huge pay-offs, and gangs fought to control it.

The Bernstein brothers and their friends from the Old Bishop School took advantage of Detroit's new status as a bootlegger's mecca and graduated from small-time hoodlums into a powerful confederation of gangsters. They began by hijacking liquor ship-ments brought into the United States by smugglers

During the early twenties, several Purples, including Ray Bern-stein, went to work for Charles Leiter and Henry Shorr, who oper-ated an outfit called the Oakland Sugar House Gang. They specialized in building distilleries and supplied booze to a network of blind pigs. The Purples provided Leiter and Shorr with muscle. They collected payments from blind pigs and illicit breweries, never hesitating to blacken a few eyes in the process.

Eventually, they diversified. Purples opened their own blind pigs and handboots. The gang's revenue skyrocketed when the Purples forced the city's bookmakers to use their wire service. They further solidified their power by forming an alliance with Egan's Rats, an outfit from St. Louis, in a gang feud over a liquor distributor. By the late 1920s, the Purple Gang ruled the Detroit underworld.

The Purples would do anything to protect their rackets, includ-ing murder. Authorities estimate that as many as five hundred unsolved homicides from Prohibition-era Detroit resulted from Pur-ple Gang activity.

In March 1927, the Purples made underworld history as one of the first gangs to use automatic weapons in a crime. The crime remains officially unsolved, but police believed that the Purples set up a meeting with one of their enemies, Frank Wright, at the Milaflores Apartments. They hired notorious gunman Fred "Killer" Burke, who would later play a role in the St. Valentine's Day Mas-sacre, to take care of business.

Just before 5 A.M. on March 28, 1927, Burke gunned down Wright and two of his associates with a Thompson submachine gun.

The attack strafed the walls with bullets—approximately 110 in total—and left the bodies of the three victims in pieces.

No one who crossed the Purples was safe, not even cops. Typically, organized crime syndicates usually left police officers alone and even went into business with flatfoots who agreed to look the other way. But they generally didn't harm them.

The Purples broke this rule when they gunned down Detroit police officer Vivian Welch in January 1928. Welch and his partner, Max Wisman, earned a little extra on the side by shaking down blind pigs, threatening them with a raid if they didn't ante up hush money. Wisman was kicked off the force, but Welch continued his dangerous sideline of extortion.

Around 1 P.M., eyewitnesses saw Welch jump out of a car and bolt down the street. Two men jumped out after him and chased the frightened cop, shooting at him as they ran. Wounded, Welch fell in the middle of the street. When the two men caught up to Welch, they stood over him and shot him in the head, execution-style. The shooters then got back into the car and fled the scene, running over Welch's body as they motored away. Police managed to trace the car to Raymond Bernstein, but no one went to trial. The crime remains officially unsolved.

Incidents like the Milaflores Massacre and the murder of Vivian Welch sent a message to rival gangs: the Purple Gang runs Detroit. The message worked. Even Al Capone wouldn't tangle with them. Capone wanted to take over Detroit but decided instead to do business with the Purples by purchasing Canadian whiskey that he sold in Chicago under his Log Cabin label.

With spectacularly violent examples made of anyone who crossed them, the Purples managed to keep other gangs in check, but like many organized crime outfits, the Purple Gang suffered from feuds among its members. One of the showdowns ended at a quiet, residential apartment complex called Collingwood Manor.

It all began with three minor crooks who wanted a larger slice of the action. Joseph Lebovitz, Herman Paul, and Isadore Sutker began as small-time hoods in Chicago. Like other Prohibition-era gangsters, they trafficked in illegal liquor and extorted money from speakeasies by forcing them to pay protection money. But by 1925, Al Capone had a firm grip on Chicago and supplied many of the speakeasies with beer. The three hoods found themselves in the dangerous position of extorting money from joints protected by Capone, so they decided to relocate.

They traveled east to Detroit, where they went to work as guns-for-hire, helping the boys from Paradise Valley climb to the top of Detroit's underworld. They became key players in the Little Jewish Navy—an arm of the Purple Gang named for its business of using boats to traffic liquor across the Detroit River. The men worked as security for the clandestine alcohol shipments that came across the river from Canada to the area between 3rd and 4th Avenues.

But Lebovitz, Paul, and Sutker decided they wanted more than side jobs as Purple muscle; they planned to carve out a piece of the prohibition boomtown for themselves. The trio began to ambush and hijack liquor shipments from Purple operators, earning the nickname "the Terrors of Third Street." They also fell into their old habit of shaking down speakeasies, this time squeezing protection money from places already protected by fellow Purples.

The Terrors later went into business with a bookie named Sol Levine and opened their own gambling racket. Business was good for a while until they didn't have the funds to pay off six-figure losses to members of another gang. So they hatched a plan to make a quick profit. They purchased whiskey from the Purple Gang on credit, cut it, and then resold the watered-down hooch for a discount price, undercutting the other alcohol distributors.

By mid-August 1931, the Terrors had become the bullies of gangland Detroit. They had stolen and extorted from the other gangs, undercut liquor prices, and they owed Ray Bernstein a large sum of money for about fifty gallons of booze—money they didn't have. The American Legion's national convention would take place in September, and the Legionnaires provided a large customer base for the town's gambling venues and blind pigs—enough profit to pay their debt to Bernstein, if the Purple gangster was willing to wait that long.

Ray Bernstein had come a long way from Paradise Valley, where he began his criminal resume by running errands for gamblers. By 1931, he found himself at the top of shadowy and vast criminal empire. A suave character known as a fine dresser and a ladykiller, Ray also had a sinister side and would use violence as a tool to get what he wanted.

The Terrors had become a thorn in Bernstein's side, so he concocted a plan to remove them from the scene, permanently. Since the Terrors never went anywhere without guards, he needed an accomplice to lure them to a "meeting." That someone, Bernstein decided, was Sol Levine.

Ray Bernstein and Solly Levine had known each other since they were kids. Levine came from a good family and even went to work in his family's business, but he began "pulling whiskey," he later said, "for the thrills." As a childhood friend of the Bernsteins and a business partner of the Terrors, Levine made the perfect go-between for a peace meeting. He also made the perfect patsy, so Ray Bernstein devised a plan to use Levine in the setup.

He told Levine that he had decided to make the Terrors his agents for alcohol distribution and racetrack betting when they paid off their debt to him. Lebovitz, Paul, and Sutker were thrilled. Their problems were over, and they would become big shots in the Detroit underworld—a role they coveted since they first came to town. The details, Bernstein told Levine, would be ironed out in a sit-down sometime in the near future.

Now that he had hooked the Terrors, Bernstein needed a place for the ambush, a quiet place that wouldn't raise any suspicion of a double cross. Under the name of "James Regis," Ray Bernstein rented apartment 211 at Collingwood Manor.

By mid-September, Bernstein was ready to spring his trap. On September 16, he contacted Levine and told him to bring Lebovitz, Paul, and Sutker to 1740 Collingwood Avenue for their meeting. Levine and the Terrors arrived at the apartment complex around 3:00

P.M. They decided that bringing weapons or guards to the meeting would be an insult, so they came unarmed. The setup had worked perfectly.

They parked their DeSoto on the street in front of the three-story brick building and went up to room 211, where they were greeted by Ray Bernstein. Three other men—Purples Harry Fleisher, Harry Keywell, and Irving Milberg—waited in the living room. They were listening to a phonograph but turned off the machine when Bernstein led the four guests into the room.

The men smoked cigars and chatted for a few minutes. Then Bernstein asked about the bookkeeper, who was apparently late for the meeting. Bernstein told the others that he was going to leave and call the bookkeeper from a store around the corner. He then walked from the apartment to the adjacent alley and revved his car's engine—a prearranged signal to Fleisher, Keywell, and Milberg.

When Fleisher heard the roaring of the car's engine, he reached into his coat and pulled out a .38. Lebovitz turned for the door, but Fleisher shot him before he could use it. Levine watched, frozen in terror, as Lebovitz fell to the floor in the hallway with a cigar clenched between his teeth.

Keywell and Milberg then pulled their .38 revolvers and fired a volley of shots at Paul and Sutker. Eight slugs hit Paul in the back, and he fell on the floor by the sofa next to Lebovitz. Sutker, who was sitting on the arm of the sofa, managed to stagger into an adjacent room in the apartment, where he tried to crawl under a bed in an attempt to shield himself from the barrage of bullets. He died on the floor with his head under the bed. The attack happened so fast, all three victims fell to the floor still clutching their cigars.

When the shooting stopped, the three gunmen approached Levine, who was trembling with fear. "Come on," Fleisher said to Levine. Ray Bernstein had ordered them not to shoot his old school chum. The four men then went into the apartment kitchen and dropped the murder weapons into a can of green paint and raced down the stairwell.

In the alley below, Ray Bernstein waited in the getaway car. Levine, Keywell, and Milberg got into the 1930 Chrysler, but Fleisher went back to the apartment. Lebovitz was still alive, he believed, so he shot him several times before joining the others.

When Fleisher returned, the group sped away from Collingwood Manor and split up. Bernstein gave Levine some money and dropped him off at his bookmaking operation. He allowed Levine to walk away from apartment 211 because he planned to frame his buddy for the triple homicide.

Meanwhile, a worried tenant who heard popping sounds followed by odd thuds on the ceiling alerted the building manager, Frank Holt. Holt found the grisly spectacle: three men lying face-down with crimson halos of blood around their heads. He shut the door and called the police, who arrived on the scene so quickly after the shootings that the victims, and the cigars they held, were still warm.

Detectives searched the apartment and discovered the bucket of green paint containing three .38 revolvers. The paint destroyed any chance of lifting fingerprints from the guns and the serial numbers had been filed off, but ballistics tests later proved that they were the murder weapons.

The police moved swiftly to catch the killers. Less than an hour after they arrived at the scene, detectives found Sol Levine, who told them that Lebovitz, Paul, and Sutker were kidnapped while en route to the rendezvous with Bernstein. Investigators didn't believe a word of Levine's story, which changed a little each time he told it.

Eventually, he broke down and abandoned the kidnapping tale. Levine fingered Fleisher, Keywell, and Milberg as the triggermen and Ray Bernstein as the one who drove the getaway car. Police threw a net over the city.

Acting on a tip, police raced to a house owned by Purple Gang lieutenant Charles Auerbach. They searched the house and found Bernstein and Keywell along with a cache of weapons and more than $9,000 in cash. The two men planned to leave the state, but investigators got to them first.

Irving Milberg also planned to skip town; however, detectives collared him the next night at fellow Purple Gang member Eddie Fletcher's apartment. Milberg was playing cards with Fletcher and another Purple named Abe Axler when police smashed through the door. They caught Milberg just as he was about to leap through a window.

Within a few days of the massacre, detectives managed to find an eyewitness to the shooting, identify the driver of the getaway car, and capture two of the three shooters. They could not, however, find the third man Levine fingered. Harry Fleisher somehow managed to escape the police dragnet and disappeared.

While authorities hunted for Fleisher, the other three Purples faced the music. With Levine as their star witness, the trial began on November 2, 1931. The state's entire case hinged on Levine's testimony, so authorities did everything in their power to keep him safe. Surrounded by four detectives, Levine took the stand and described what happened inside of apartment 211. Levine testified that he believed the meeting was arranged to settle the debt the three men owed Bernstein. He was just as shocked as the victims when he discovered that Bernstein had used him as the lure in an assassination plot.

The defense attacked Sol Levine's credibility, but the weight of the bookmaker's testimony crushed Bernstein, Keywell, and Milberg. In his closing statement, the prosecutor summarized the motive for the murders, noting that the three men had used blood instead of red ink for their ledgers.

After deliberating for just over ninety minutes, the jury returned its verdict: all three men were guilty of first-degree murder. A week later, they were sentenced to life in prison and transported to a penitentiary in Michigan's Upper Peninsula. The Purple Gang had lost three of its key players, including one of its chiefs.

While the three Purples traveled to their new home in Marquette, Sol Levine took a trip in a different direction. He believed the Purples put a price on his head. "I don't intend to stand around and wait to be put on the spot," Levine told reporters. "I'm getting out of

Detroit, maybe out of the country and I'm going to make a fresh start."

Fearing reprisals against the bookmaker, detectives escorted Levine out of Michigan.

At some point during his journey, Levine apparently had a change of heart about his trial testimony. In March 1932, the Purples' defense team presented the court with a piece of shocking new evidence that supposedly came from, of all people, Sol Levine. In a sworn affidavit, he alleged that Detroit police officers beat him into fingering Ray Bernstein, Harry Fleisher, Harry Keywell, and Irving Milberg for the Collingwood Manor Massacre. If he didn't, they threatened, he would face a jury for the murders.

The convicted murderers' defense attorneys attempted to use Levine's allegations to leverage a new trial, and their case gained momentum when a surprise visitor appeared at the district attorney's office in Detroit.

Nine months after the Collingwood Manor Massacre, Harry Fleisher surfaced. Detectives didn't run him to ground in a safe house or find him hiding in a dark corner of a blind pig; he simply walked into police headquarters in Detroit and surrendered. He came forward, he said, to help free Bernstein, Keywell, and Milberg. He had an alibi that refuted Levine's testimony and suggested that his confederates were innocent as well.

The real reason Fleisher surrendered, prosecutors believed, was because they no longer had a witness against him. Levine had dropped out of sight. While detectives searched for the Purple bookmaker, prosecutors prepared their case against Fleisher for his role in the murders.

Detectives and FBI agents grilled Fleisher about his association with the Purple Gang, his role in the Collingwood Manor Massacre, and his possible involvement in one of the era's most notorious crimes: the kidnapping of the Lindbergh baby.

The child of the famous aviator went missing on March 1, 1932, while Fleisher was on the lam. Fleisher also had a history of kidnapping. In 1930, he was arrested in connection with the kidnapping of a Connecticut realtor named Max Price. Price later identified Harry Fleisher as one of his kidnappers, but Fleisher beat the rap when eyewitnesses would not testify against him.

During exhaustive questioning by local and federal authorities, Fleisher denied any involvement in the Lindbergh kidnapping or the Collingwood Manor Massacre, claiming that he spent the night of September 16, 1931, in a Reading, Pennsylvania, jail under the name of Harry Fishman and was released on the morning of September 17. The Purples' defense attorneys argued that if Fleisher wasn't in Detroit gunning down the Terrors, as Levine had testified, then Levine's testimony about the others became questionable.

But under scrutiny, Fleisher's alibi couldn't hold water. Police records from Reading contained a signature that matched Fleisher's, but when examined closely, the documents appeared to have been doctored at a later date. A guard who worked at the Reading jail told investigators that a detective asked him to fill out an arrest ticket, leave the signature blank, and back date it to September 16, 1931. The same guard also insisted that Harry Fleisher was never in the Reading jail.

Investigators found another eyewitness who refuted Fleisher's claim. A Detroit cop saw Fleisher in Detroit on the morning of September 17, 1931, about the same time that Fleisher claimed he was leaving the Reading jail as Harry Fishman. Fleisher's alibi, it appeared, was nothing but a fish story.

The key to keeping Fleisher off the streets would be Sol Levine, but by September 1932, he was still missing. Detectives could not find the bookie, which led to a legal battle about whether or not his testimony in the original Collingwood Manor Massacre trial could now be used in proceedings against Fleisher. Under state and federal laws, the accused has a right to confront his accuser, which would not be possible without a live witness. The district attorney had no choice but to dismiss the murder charge against Fleisher.

Harry Fleisher had outsmarted the law, but the other three Purples wouldn't be so lucky. Fleisher's fishy alibi and Levine's affidavit did not convince Judge Van Zile, who characterized Levine's story of coercion as incredible and denied the three Purples a new trial in 1933.

Solly Levine did eventually surface in the early 1960s after thirty years of living in fear. He stuck to his story that the police had railroaded the three Purples, but his allegations fell on deaf ears and the Purples remained behind bars.

Milberg spent just a few years in a cell. In 1938, he died from peritonitis following an abdominal surgery. The other convicted shooter, Keywell, did thirty-four years in prison for his role in the massacre and then was released for good conduct. Time apparently straightened out the gangster. He married and spent the rest of his life as a law-abiding citizen. He died in 1997.

Bernstein remained a powerful figure, even when behind bars. He ran a gambling ring inside the big house in Jackson, and one jailhouse stool pigeon told investigators that Bernstein and Keywell left prison and assassinated Michigan state senator Warren Hooper, an allegation never proven. Hooper's murder remains unsolved.

Still, Bernstein did do some good while in prison. The former grammar school delinquent earned a high school diploma and taught school to other convicts. But his career as a prison teacher was cut short in 1963, when he suffered a stroke that left him partially paralyzed and confined to a wheelchair. A year later, in 1964, a prison board granted Bernstein a mercy parole. He died in 1966 at the University of Michigan Medical Center.

Fleisher was never convicted for his alleged role in the Collingwood Manor Massacre, but he did a four-year stint in Alcatraz for violating IRS laws. He was released in 1940, but a few years later, he was convicted for separate charges of conspiracy to commit murder and armed robbery. Like Bernstein, he managed to do some good while in prison—he donated thirty-nine pints of blood during prison blood drives. Fleisher was eventually released in 1965 and worked for a Detroit steel company before he died in 1978.

From their cells, the Purple gangsters had watched their empire collapse. Prohibition ended in 1933, and rumrunners, blind pig operators, and still-makers—the basis of the Gang's supremacy—

went out of business as the nation abandoned the "noble experiment." At ten cents for a glass of beer and twenty cents for a shot of whiskey, it didn't pay to ferry booze across the river anymore.

According to Chief Fred Frahm—a tough-as-nails Detroit cop during the Purple reign—a combination of the Collingwood Massacre trial outcome and the repeal of Prohibition led to the gang's demise. "The Purple Gang has been smashed," Frahm remarked in 1935. "The law finished the work started by jealousies between members."

Purple Gang activity would continue throughout the mid-1930s as some of the boys turned their focus to narcotics smuggling, but one by one, Purples began to disappear from the streets of Detroit, many of them victims of their own mob.

In 1933, Abe Axlar and Eddie Fletcher, two high-ranking Purples, were executed by fellow gang members. In 1934, Henry Shorr, who along with Charles Leiter ran the Oakland Sugar House Gang, disappeared. He left for a business meeting and vanished, never to be seen again. Police believe that he was also murdered by fellow Purples.

## CHAPTER 7

# Lonely Hearts:
# The Michigan Victims of
# Beck and Fernandez

In the 1940s, divorcees, widowers, and other forlorn souls turned to Lonely Hearts Clubs to meet people. They answered personal ads, wrote letters to each other, and then met in person. This was dangerous business. "When you play the lonely heart clubs wild," the *Grand Rapids Herald* warned, "you must practice a certain amount of caution."

The ominous warning was posted in the *Herald*'s March 2, 1949, front-page story detailing the capture of Beck and Fernandez, the "Lonely Hearts Killers," in Grand Rapids. The story of this killer couple, who chose their victims from Lonely Heart Club advertisements, shocked the nation. They committed crimes in several states, but their spree of deception, fraud, and murder ended in Wyoming Township, a suburb of Grand Rapids.

✳ ✳ ✳

Some say that charm and a nice smile will open just about any door. If true, there were very few doors closed to Raymond Martinez Fernandez, except the one of his Sing Sing prison cell when the law finally ended his run of deception and murder.

Fernandez was born on December 17, 1914, on the big island of Hawaii, but when he was a toddler, his family moved to the United States. As a boy, Fernandez was skinny and awkward, but by the time he reached his teens, he had developed into a handsome, soft-spoken man with charisma and charm that many women found irresistible. But the attractive youth was far from perfect; at fifteen, he was caught stealing a neighbor's chickens and did a brief stint in jail.

In 1932, at eighteen, Fernandez relocated to Spain where he worked on an uncle's farm near the village of Orgiva. He fell in love with a local woman named Encarnación Robles, and a few years later, the two wed and had a son (they eventually had four children together).

But Fernandez seemed to suffer from wanderlust. He later admitted that after a short period of marriage, he left his family and traveled to the United States to find work, but his stay was cut short by bad news from home. When he heard that his young son was seriously ill, he returned to Spain. He planned to leave the country again, but by this time the Spanish Civil War had broken out, stranding him. Fernandez fought for Franco and the Nationalists during the struggle. After the conflict, he took a series of menial jobs, including work as a gardener.

During World War II, Fernandez went to work for Spain's merchant marine and then later for British intelligence. While little is known about his brief career as a spy, he later said that it had something to do with investigating the sabotage of ships. His good looks and charm may have been powerful weapons in the secret war, and he earned a reputation in the intelligence community as a top-notch agent.

When the war ended, Fernandez planned to return to the United States. Some sources say he wanted to abandon his family, while others report that he intended to work until he earned enough money to send for them. Fernandez's trip took a tragic turn. While on a freighter crossing the Atlantic, he had a terrible accident. A steel hatch dropped on his head, fracturing his skull. The life-threatening injury landed Fernandez in a hospital bed for several weeks.

Three months later, Fernandez emerged from the hospital a very different person both mentally and physically. The once upbeat, sociable Fernandez became sullen, temperamental, and solitary. He suffered from excruciating headaches. His appearance had also changed. He had lost much of his hair, and the accident left a large scar on top of his head that he would later conceal with a toupee.

Once he recovered, Fernandez booked passage on a U.S. naval vessel headed to Mobile, Alabama. When the ship arrived, he was caught stealing items from the ship's store and sentenced to five months in a Florida federal prison. There he shared a cell with a Haitian who practiced Vodun, often referred to as Voodoo.

The mystique of Vodun, with its magic charms and spells, was alluring to Fernandez, and he became hooked on it. He studied books like *The Magic Island* by William Seabrook and became convinced that he could use Voodoo charms to seduce women from afar, especially if he possessed some personal token like a strand of hair or an earring. Fernandez was about to put his charms—both his charisma and the Voodoo he learned in prison—to work.

A model prisoner, Fernandez was given time off his sentence for good behavior. He left prison on September 30, 1946, and traveled to New York, where he stayed with relatives. There, he spent hours alone, pouring over lonely hearts classified ads.

Over the next few months, Fernandez perfected his scheme. He selected women who appeared to have substantial assets and then baited them with his articulate and romantic letters. "I asked the women about their home towns, what they were like, what their hobbies were, and so on," Fernandez said when describing his appeal to his lonely hearts victims.

"I wrote letters to about 50 women," Fernandez later explained. "I told about myself and said I was a New Yorker of independent means." After establishing a relationship through correspondence, Fernandez typically requested a personal memento so he could perform a Voodoo ritual that he believed would make the woman unable to resist him. Then, the two lonely hearts would meet, become intimate, and Fernandez would fleece his paramours of anything with value.

It was easy business for a conman like Fernandez. The older, lonely ladies that he selected from the personals devoured the attention of an attractive, younger man. One of these women was Jane Thompson. A recent separation left her lonely and vulnerable, and she began corresponding with Fernandez. They took a cruise to Spain in October 1947 and spent the next few weeks touring the country. Fernandez was a gifted con artist; he even introduced Thompson to his Spanish wife, Encarnación Robles, who appeared to accept the fact that her husband had taken a lover.

Then, on November 17, 1947, something went wrong. That night, Fernandez was seen leaving a hotel room he shared with Thompson after what investigators believed was a heated argument. Thompson's body was discovered the next morning. Authorities initially believed that she died as a result of an intestinal parasite and buried her body without an autopsy.

Later, when investigators suspected that Fernandez may have poisoned Thompson, they wanted to question him, but he was long gone. He had returned to New York, where he appeared at Thompson's apartment with a forged will that bequeathed the property to him. He told Thompson's elderly mother, who lived in the apartment, that her daughter died in a train wreck.

Meanwhile, he had already established correspondence with his next mark, a nurse from Florida named Martha Beck. It didn't take much to seduce Beck, who also found Fernandez's attention irresistible. When she first met him, Beck was twenty-eight and the mother of two children from two disastrous relationships. Her weight—well over 200 pounds—crimped her personal life, and she spent hours reading romance magazines and dreaming of Mr. Right.

Beck was born Martha Jule Seabrook in the town of Milton, Florida, on May 6, 1920. She always struggled with her weight and grew up with constant ridicule from friends and her domineering mother, who watched her every move, particularly when it came to boys and dating.

In 1942, she graduated from a Florida nursing school at the top of her class. She got a job at a local mortuary for a while, but World War II had begun and nurses were needed on the West Coast, so Martha moved to California where she went to work at an Army base. She enjoyed the local nightlife and the companionship of the soldiers on leave, and before long she got pregnant. Despite her pleas, the father refused to marry her, so pregnant and alone, Martha returned to Florida.

To avoid a possible scandal, she concocted a cover story to explain the pregnancy to the people back home. She said that while in California, she married an officer in the U.S. Navy named Joe Carmen who had returned to duty in the Pacific. The story was convincing, and Beck went to extraordinary measures to maintain her ruse. She bought herself a wedding ring and told neighbors that she couldn't wait for her husband to return.

But her fictitious husband would never return, a fact that Martha established when she sent herself a telegram notifying her of her husband's death. Martha played the role of bereaved widow to an audience of sympathetic friends and family. And she played the role well: the local newspaper even ran a story about her loss.

It didn't take the young widow long to find love again. In 1944, just after the birth of her daughter Willa Dean, Martha fell for a bus driver named Alfred Beck. Once again, she got pregnant out of wedlock, but this time, she wouldn't need to make up a husband to explain—Beck decided to marry her. The Becks' marriage didn't make it past the honeymoon phase. After just six months, the pair split, leaving Martha with two young children and no means to support them.

Now "widowed" and divorced with two young children, Martha was lonely and unemployed, but she managed to scrape by for a while. Then in 1946, her life took a turn for the better. She found a nursing job at a Florida children's hospital, where she eventually worked her way up to nurse superintendent. But Beck was lonely, so in 1947, she paid $5 to join Mother Dinene's Friendly Club for Lonely Hearts and placed a personal ad. She received just one reply, from a New Yorker named Raymond Fernandez.

In his initial letter to Beck, Fernandez wrote, "Why did I choose you for my debut friendship letter? Because you are a nurse and therefore I know you have a full heart with a great capacity for comfort and love." The real reason Fernandez chose Beck was because he thought that, as a nurse, Beck would have substantial assets. Fernandez also noticed a stunning coincidence. Beck's maiden name was Seabrook—the same name as the author of *The Magic Island*, a book on Voodoo and the source of the spells that Fernandez believed he could use to seduce his victims from afar.

For the next two weeks, the pair exchanged letters. In one, Fernandez asked Beck to send him a lock of her hair The request titillated Beck, who eagerly sent a few strands in her next letter. Fernandez wanted a personal item to cast a Voodoo spell that he believed would make Beck powerless to resist him.

With the ritual performed, Fernandez traveled to Florida a few days after Christmas 1947, and the two began a torrid but short-lived affair. When Fernandez discovered that Beck had few assets that he could steal, he retreated to New York and wrote another letter to end the relationship.

Beck was crushed. Unable to accept the breakup, she traveled to New York. Fernandez reluctantly let her stay with him in the apartment he swindled from Jane Thompson, and the couple continued their affair for two weeks.

When Beck returned to Florida, she discovered that the children's hospital had fired her without cause, possibly because of her relationship with Fernandez. She packed a few things, and with her two children in tow, caught the next bus to New York City. Fernandez allowed Beck to stay, but not her kids. It was a sacrifice that she was willing to make for the lover of her dreams. In January 1948, a week after she arrived, Beck left her children with the Salvation Army and returned to Fernandez's apartment, where she learned the truth about her lover and his lonely-hearts scam.

The pair decided that they could work the confidence game as a team with Beck posing as Fernandez's sister or sister-in-law. They studied the personal advertisements for potential marks and began correspondence. Beck even wrote a few of the letters, which Fernandez signed with the pen name "Charles Martin."

It is unclear why Beck became such a willing accomplice in her lover's criminal enterprise. She later told authorities that she would do anything for Fernandez; his wish was her command. Some speculate that Beck, after years of swallowing comments about her weight, was happy to exact a little revenge by stealing from other women.

Over the next few months, Beck and Fernandez worked their game. They traveled throughout the country meeting lonely hearts—mostly older widows. Beck played the role of caring sister or sister-in-law, while Fernandez charmed and seduced the ladies. They convinced the gullible women to liquidate or sign over assets and then moved on to their next target. From January 1948 until their capture in March 1949, they conned numerous women, two of whom Fernandez married, making him a bigamist as well as a thief (and he was still married to Encarnción Robles).

Beck played her role well and gave the enterprise an appearance of credibility, but jealousy began to consume her. This was supposed to be business, not pleasure. She rejected younger correspondents because she didn't want Fernandez to enjoy his work and did whatever she could to prevent the relationships from becoming intimate. Sometimes she succeeded, sometimes she didn't.

On August 14, 1948, Fernandez married a forty-year-old widow named Myrtle Young in Cook County, Illinois. Beck once again played the sister, but this time she went to extraordinary lengths to keep the newlyweds apart. She even slept in the same bed as Young on the pretense that the groom was shy.

The marriage was short-lived. Following an argument about $1,600 and a car Fernandez took from Young, the con artists fed her a large dose of barbiturates that left her in a stupor. They put Young on a bus headed to her hometown of Little Rock, Arkansas. When the bus arrived, she was nearly unconscious. Police took her to a local hospital and a few days later she died of what was presumed to be a cerebral hemorrhage and inflammation of the liver.

Their next major mark was Janet Fay, a sixty-six-year-old widow from Albany, New York. Beck and Fernandez arrived in Albany on December 30, 1948, and within a week, Fernandez and the unsuspecting woman were engaged. Fay spent the first few days of January closing her accounts. On January 4, with her banking completed and a bankroll of $6,000, Fay traveled to Long Island with Beck and Fernandez.

The relationship ended as fast as it began. Sometime that night an argument, possibly motivated by Beck's intense jealousy of Fay, erupted between the two women. Beck smashed Fay in the head with a hammer, and Fernandez garroted her with a scarf. They put Fay's body in a large trunk and then drove it to the home of Fernandez's sister, who knew nothing of the murder or of the corpse inside the chest that was now sitting in her basement. A week and a half later, Beck and Fernandez took the trunk to a home they rented in Queens and buried the body in the cellar. Fernandez then sealed Fay's makeshift grave with a layer of cement.

The con, though, wasn't quite over yet. While Beck and Fernandez waited for the cement to harden, they typed letters to Fay's family in her name. In the forged letters, Fay describes her happiness with the prospect of becoming Mrs. Charles Martin and requests that they send some of her things to New York.

When the cement over Janet Fay dried, the Lonely Hearts Killers traveled to Grand Rapids, Michigan. There they met their next victim, a twenty-eight-year-old widow named Deliphene Price Downing, whom Fernandez had corresponded with over the past few weeks while he and Beck met, fleeced, and then murdered Janet Fay.

Price grew up on a 3,200-acre farm near Palisade, Nebraska. At 17, she began teaching at a local school. In the summer of 1942, she traveled west to visit one of her sisters in Los Angeles. During this visit, she met a young soldier from Grand Rapids named Rolland Downing. Deliphene returned to Nebraska, but they continued their romance through the mail. They married in 1944 while Rolland was on leave.

When Rolland left the military in 1945, the couple moved to Grand Rapids, where Rolland went to work as a truck driver for a local lumber company. The newlyweds purchased a small home in Wyoming Township, a suburban community southwest of the city.

In November 1947, just five months after the birth of his daughter Rainell, Rolland died in a tragic accident. A train collided with his truck, hurling him from the driver's seat. After Rolland's death, Deliphene and Rainell managed to survive on a meager monthly insurance payment of $125 a month.

Friends and relatives described "Dela" as quiet but friendly and cheerful, often conversing with neighbors who passed by her home. Loneliness, though, took its toll on the young widow, and she joined a lonely hearts club. She placed an ad and received a response from a well-to-do New Yorker named Charles Martin.

Fernandez and Beck, as Martin and his twenty-nine-year-old sister, arrived in Grand Rapids on January 23, 1949. Fernandez worked his charms, and within days, they moved into Downing's home at 3435 Byron Center Road. "I liked her better than any of the other women," Fernandez later said, and described Downing as "really an honest woman."

Over the next few weeks, Beck and Fernandez worked their confidence game. Fernandez told Downing that he would take her back to New York and marry her, so the enraptured widow began to make plans for her new life. She and Fernandez established a joint savings account. Fernandez deposited $2,700 and Downing, $1,300. She also sold her house and received a $500 down payment, arranging for the payments to be sent to New York, where she believed the soon-to-be newlyweds would live.

The future bride, excited with the prospect of becoming Mrs. Martin, and perhaps wanting to avoid the appearance of intimacy before vows, told others that a marriage had already occurred. On February 2, they threw a party and served wedding cake. Then they traveled to Nebraska to visit Dela's parents. Beck played the role of a nurse who helped deliver Rainell and then later introduced Dela to her new beau. Fernandez played the role of the suave newlywed, Dela the love-struck bride. But only Beck and Fernandez were acting; Dela was hooked, convinced that her days of loneliness were history.

The fictitious honeymoon abruptly ended three weeks later. Like the Fay murder, there are differing accounts of what happened next and why. According to the confession Beck and Fernandez gave to Michigan authorities, on Saturday, February 27, 1949, Fernandez came home wearing a new toupee he bought in Grand Rapids. Shocked at his changed appearance, Dela became suspicious and accused him of deceiving her. The argument turned to finances, and Dela accused Fernandez of attempting to defraud her. She was enraged and the argument became violent, Fernandez later told investigators. Dela began throwing pots and pans at him.

He turned to Beck for help. "Fernandez asked me if I had enough sleeping pills to put her out of the way for good," she later confessed. "I thought I had as I had 14 one and a half grain phenobarbital pills." Dela didn't want to take the pills, but Beck reminded her that she was a trained nurse and convinced her to swallow them.

Dela fell into a deep stupor. Later that evening, she tried to get out of bed but was too drugged. According to Beck, at this point, Fernandez decided to murder her. He wrapped a .45 in two of Rainell's blankets to muffle the sound and shot Dela in the head. While Beck attempted to wrap up the body with a blanket and some rope, Fernandez went to the basement to dig a grave.

He dug for a few hours. When he finished, he and Beck carried Dela's body to the basement, but the hole had filled with muddy water. Beck bailed the water with a small washtub and they placed the body in the hole, which Fernandez then covered with plaster of paris that he had bought from a local hardware store under the guise that he was doing some home repairs.

With the job done, they cleaned up and took Rainell to a movie as if nothing had happened. The next day, Sunday, they bought Rainell a puppy, which they later returned because it scratched her.

On Monday, however, Beck and Fernandez decided to murder the child, too. Rainell's crying woke them that morning, and they realized that the little girl would become a liability, so they discussed "putting it down with its mother," Fernandez later said. According to Beck, Fernandez asked her to smother the child, but she told him she couldn't do it. He couldn't either, he said. While they mulled it over, Beck and Fernandez made plans to skip town. They went to the bank to withdraw the money from the joint account that Fernandez and Downing established, and when they returned to Downing's home, Beck decided to drown Rainell.

She carried the naked child to the basement and held Rainell by the heels, shoving her head into the tub of muddy water bailed from the hole. Rainell struggled, so Beck used her weight as leverage, forcing the toddler's head into the mud. Fernandez heard crying and ran to the basement, but the sight of the infant's head in the tub sent him back up the stairs.

When Fernandez recovered his composure, he returned to the basement. They placed Rainell's body in a small, green box and left it on the cellar floor. And then, once again, they went to the movies.

When they returned Monday night, a knock at their door brought a surprise: four police officers. Dela hadn't been seen outside of her home since Friday, and concerned neighbors called her father-in-law, Ralph Downing, who notified the police.

Beck and Fernandez had a cover story to explain the widow's absence: Dela took Rainell to Detroit, Beck and Fernandez told the officers. But the cops noticed something fishy—packed luggage. A search of Fernandez revealed a bankroll of over $4,000, and the suave New Yorker couldn't explain the large sum of money he had on him. So the police took Beck and Fernandez to a local jail for questioning.

Meanwhile, officers searched the house. In the basement, they found a suspicious sight: a wet patch of concrete with pipes jutting out of it as if someone had attempted a crude plumbing job. So they cleared a few things out of the way, including a green box the size of a footlocker, and began digging. For about two hours they labored in the cramped cellar, alternately chipping at the cement and bailing the water that welled up in the hole. A few feet under the surface, they found the body of Deliphene Downing.

But they did not find Rainell, so they returned to jail to question Fernandez. Where could they find the child? "In the little green box," he told them, and they returned to the house. They opened the box and found Rainell trussed up with wire and covered by a pink baby blanket. The medical examiner later determined that Rainell hadn't drowned but instead suffocated when Beck held her head in the watery mud.

Beck and Fernandez were taken to the Kent County Jail. Faced with two murders, they admitted everything. During lengthy interviews that resulted in a seventy-three-page confession, Beck and Fernandez narrated the sordid tale of their lonely hearts racket. They had nothing to lose. In Michigan, they did not face a death penalty. In New York, first-degree murder carried a mandatory sentence of death by electrocution.

The Lonely Hearts Killers outlined their confidence game: the way they chose their victims, the methods used to con lonely women out of their savings, and the details of the murders of Janet Fay and Deliphene and Rainell Downing. Investigators and prosecutors listened, mouths agape, as the two described the murder of twenty-one-month-old Rainell.

When they returned from the bank on Monday, Beck took Rainell down to the basement to drown her. "In a little while," Fernandez said, "I heard her crying and ran down and said, 'Let her be, don't make her suffer anymore.'" When he saw the child headfirst in the tub, he couldn't stand the sight and darted back up the stairs. "What's the matter, why don't you come down?" Beck yelled up the stairs, taunting him, Fernandez said.

In a cold, emotionless tone, Beck gave a chilling account of Rainell's murder. "The baby struggled so much I could hardly hold her," Beck said. "So, I wrapped it in a blanket and held it all the way under for fifteen or twenty minutes."

They also described the murder of Janet Fay in New York. Beck admitted to bashing the sixty-six-year-old widow in the head with a hammer, and Fernandez confessed to strangling her with a scarf. Beck described the grisly scene to stunned detectives: When Fernandez garroted Fay, the elderly woman's dentures fell out. The killers then explained how they disposed of Fay's body.

Fernandez hinted at a motive for the three murders. Beck, he explained, became jealous of his attentions to both Fay and Downing. Beck, however, offered a different explanation. She said they were not premeditated but were done because the women had become suspicious and a threat to their scam. "I didn't kill in a jealous mood," Beck said. "It was more self-preservation." Kent County prosecutor Roger McMahon believed that the motive for the Michigan murders was simple greed; Beck and Fernandez killed Deliphene Downing because she planned to send $1,500 to her family, a significant portion of Fernandez's take in the scam.

Grand Rapids authorities relayed the information about Janet Fay's murder to New York investigators, who broke through the concrete of the basement in Queens and found Fay's body. The authorities initiated proceedings to extradite the two killers, which meant that Beck and Fernandez could go to the electric chair.

By sheer coincidence, at the same time Beck and Fernandez were outlining their fifteen-month crime spree, the Michigan legislature was debating the reinstatement of a death penalty with the Betz-Warner electric chair bill. One death penalty advocate mentioned the Downing murder during the debate, but it didn't make a difference. The death penalty bill was defeated in the Michigan House. Michigan murderers would not face the electric chair for their crimes.

But the Lonely Hearts killers would. Beck and Fernandez were on their way to New York. Michigan authorities delayed trial proceedings long enough to allow New York prosecutors the time they needed to extradite them for the murder of Janet Fay.

The trial began in June 1949 and lasted through mid-August. It created a nationwide sensation and supplied the newspapers with daily headlines as the two confessed killers spoke in front of a packed courtroom.

During his testimony, Fernandez detailed his sexual relationships with Martha Beck and his various victims. Fernandez also attempted to retract the confession he gave in Michigan, claiming that he only said he helped murder Janet Fay to protect Beck. He admitted twisting a scarf around Fay's neck to stop the bleeding, but he now claimed that the widow was already dead when he got there. Even though he tried to worm his way out of a direct role in the New York slaying, on cross-examination, Fernandez did admit to murdering Deliphene Downing in Michigan.

Like her partner, Beck provided the New York media with plenty of juicy headlines. On her way to the stand, heavily made up with vibrant red lipstick, she took a detour to Raymond. She held his face in her hands and kissed him, leaving him streaked with lipstick. Guards pulled the two apart and she began her testimony.

Beck professed her love for Fernandez and said that she would do anything for him. She gave a detailed account of her sexual relations with him and the Voodoo rituals the two performed together.

As for the murder of Janet Fay, Beck's defense attempted to show that Beck, in a fit of insanity caused by intense jealousy, struck Fay. During the murder, Beck testified, she blacked out. She went into a daze and the next thing she remembered, she was standing over Fay, who was lying on the floor bleeding. Beck also offered the

ridiculous explanation—perhaps an attempt to shield her lover—
that she instructed Fernandez to wrap a scarf around Fay's neck,
tourniquet-style, to stop the bleeding.

But the jury had also heard testimony from Michigan authorities
who described the graphic details of the confession Beck and Fernandez signed, which included the murder of Janet Fay. Three
weeks and 45,000 pages of testimony later, the jury found both
Beck and Fernandez guilty of first-degree murder—a verdict that
carried a mandatory sentence of death in the electric chair.

The racket had ended, but the love letters didn't. The two con-
tinued their romance through notes sent to each other from Sing
Sing's death row. Fernandez also wrote several letters to his wife in
Spain, declaring his love for her.

The Lonely Hearts Killers both took the long walk to Sing
Sing's electric chair on March 8, 1951. Raymond Fernandez went
first. Just before the execution, Beck sent him one final love letter,
which appeared to steel her partner in crime. "I'll die like a man,"
he said after he read the note, but he collapsed while walking to the
chair. Guards carried him the rest of the way.

Beck followed her lover twelve minutes later. In her last statement to the press, she said, "My story is a love story . . . in the history of the world, how many crimes have been attributed to love?"

Just how many murders Beck and Fernandez committed is a
question without a definite answer. Myrtle Young is a probable
fourth victim. If Fernandez poisoned Jane Thompson in Spain, she
becomes his fifth victim. But there could be others. Some place the
total as high as a dozen. The real number may never be known.

Beck and Fernandez fleeced dozens of women during their
Lonely Hearts racket. When the pair was arrested in Grand Rapids,
investigators found among Raymond Fernandez's belongings a list
containing sixteen names of women in twelve states that they
believed were his future victims. A news report from the *Chicago
Tribune* placed the number of Fernandez's past and future contacts
as high as 132.

These numbers suggest that for many lonely ladies of the 1940s, playing the lonely heart clubs was dangerous business. Even Martha Beck acknowledged this fact when she confessed to Michigan detectives. "Why don't you put an end to these matrimonial bureaus?" she asked. "They're nothing but rackets."

# CHAPTER 8
# The Ypsi Coed Killer

U.S. Highway 23 divides the towns of Ypsilanti and Ann Arbor and their two universities. A drive down Washtenaw Avenue, the east-west artery that connects the two campuses, will take the traveler from the fringe of the University of Michigan's Central Campus to the humorously phallic-looking water tower at the gateway of Eastern Michigan University. In the late 1960s, a predator traveled down Washtenaw, stalking co-eds on both campuses. The media dubbed this person "The Coed Killer."

On July 26, 1969, a doctor and his wife stumbled upon a grisly scene on the way to their mailbox. In a tree-covered ditch off of Riverside Drive in Ann Arbor, they found the nude body of a young girl, battered beyond recognition. The girl had met a gruesome fate. She was beaten, raped, and strangled.

The autopsy revealed that the victim suffered unseen indignities. During the postmortem, the coroner discovered the victim's torn underwear lodged inside her vagina. The panties contained a vital clue that could tie the victim to her murderer: hair clippings from another person. Not hairs, but hair clippings—an odd clue that suggested she may have been murdered in or around a barbershop. Fingerprints identified the victim as eighteen-year-old Karen Sue Beineman, a college student from Grand Rapids.

Beineman was taking summer classes at Eastern Michigan University when she disappeared on July 23, 1969. She had been last seen at a wig shop in downtown Ypsilanti. Beineman told the store clerk that she had done two foolish things in her life. One was buying a wig, and the other was hitching a ride with a stranger—a man waiting outside the shop on a motorcycle. These were the coed's last words, and they proved to be tragically prophetic. Four days later, she surfaced in a gully, the seventh victim of what appeared to be a serial killer preying on young coeds.

The first murder occurred about two years earlier. On August 7, 1967, two farm boys found the nude body of nineteen-year-old Mary Fleszar lying by the foundation of an old house. Her body was badly decomposed and missing one hand, all the fingers of the other, and both feet. Broken leg bones indicated that her killer beat her savagely before stabbing her an estimated thirty times. It appeared that the killer had murdered her elsewhere and weeks later dumped her at this spot, about three miles from her apartment. He later returned to this scene and moved her body, possibly a few times.

Fleszar, an accounting student at EMU, disappeared almost a month earlier when she went out for a walk. Sometime during her evening stroll, she came across an attractive young man who offered her a ride. An eyewitness, who later described the incident to investigators, watched as a blue-gray Chevy pulled up to her. The driver, an unidentified young man, spoke to Fleszar, who shook her head and kept walking. The driver approached her again, and once again she walked away. The driver then pulled away and

Fleszar continued walking. She wasn't seen again until her body was found in August.

Curiously, a young man driving a blue-gray Chevy visited the funeral home handling Fleszar's remains and asked if he could take a photograph of her body. The funeral home immediately denied the morbid request. Unfortunately, no one at the funeral home could give the police a definitive description of the man.

Almost a year after Fleszar's murder, another EMU coed disappeared. Twenty-year-old Joan Schell was hitchhiking on the evening of June 30, 1968. That night, an eyewitness saw Schell climb into a car with three unidentified men. That was the last time anyone saw the pretty coed alive.

A week later, on July 6, 1968, construction workers found Schell's body just a few miles away from the where the farm boys discovered Fleszar's remains. Schell had been stabbed twenty-five times and her blue miniskirt was tied around her neck. Police estimated that Schell, like Fleszar, was killed in another spot and moved. Sometime in the past twenty-four hours, Schell's killer had deposited her body in a place where it was sure to be found.

Police questioned Schell's boyfriend, who passed a lie-detector test, and another man, a twenty-one-year-old EMU education major named John Norman Collins. The boyishly handsome Collins had come under suspicion because he had been seen with Schell the night she disappeared and later described, in graphic detail, Schell's injuries to female co-workers. Collins had an alibi, though; he told police that he spent June 30, the day Schell disappeared, with his mother in the Detroit area, and he wished them well in their hunt for Schell's killer.

Nine months later, police discovered the body of yet another coed. On March 21, 1969, the body of a twenty-three-year-old Michigan law student named Jane Mixer turned up in a cemetery. Like Joan Schell, Mixer had an item of clothing—in this case a stocking—around her neck. But unlike the other two women, Mixer had been shot twice in the head and was left fully clothed in an area distant from the other two locations. And unlike the other two, there was no evidence that Mixer had been sexually assaulted.

Police had a promising lead in the Mixer case. Just before her murder, Mixer supposedly arranged for a ride from Ann Arbor to Muskegon, her hometown, with a David Johnson. A student at the University of Michigan's law school, Mixer obtained the ride by posting a note on a bulletin board at the university—a form of ride sharing common at the time. Police interviewed several David Johnsons, all of whom had alibis. David Johnson, it appeared, was a pseudonym.

The mysterious name wasn't their only clue. In the basement of a campus dormitory, police found a telephone book with a handwritten notation on its cover—the name "Mixer" and the misspelling of her hometown, "Muskegeon." This would prove one of the keys in the case against Mixer's murderer. But for now, it was a dead end.

By this time, residents began to question if the three murders were somehow related. There were similarities in the first two cases. Fleszar and Schell were young, female, and brunette EMU students. Both had been sexually molested, stabbed, and then dumped days after their deaths in spots where they were sure to be discovered. The murders occurred almost a year apart. Mixer's murder, nine months later, differed from the other two in several ways. So at this point, investigators still considered the three as separate cases.

Then, a few days after Jane Mixer's body turned up, everything changed. The discovery of three more victims during the spring of 1969 convinced residents and investigators alike that the murders were connected. The possibility of a serial killer stalking coeds of the two universities terrorized locals and captured headlines throughout the state.

On March 25, 1969, the body of sixteen-year-old Maralynn Skelton was found in an Ann Arbor subdivision just a few hundred yards from where construction workers had found the body of Joan Schell. The day before, Skelton, a high school dropout from Romulus, was hitchhiking on Washtenaw Avenue outside of the Arbor-land Mall. When she didn't show up to meet a friend on EMU's campus, her parents contacted the police.

Skelton had been severely beaten and tortured. Marks on her chest indicated that her killer used restraints to hold her down while he whipped her legs with a leather belt. The left side of her face was battered and her skull shattered by repeated blows from a blunt object. There was a garter belt tied around her neck and a tree branch inserted eight inches into her vagina. To muffle the young girl's screams, the killer had jammed a swatch of cloth down her throat.

Police barely had enough time to follow up on their leads when another girl went missing. Just two weeks after Maralynn Skelton, thirteen-year-old Dawn Basom, a middle school student from Ypsilanti, disappeared. She was last seen walking in Ypsilanti at dusk on April 15, 1969. An eyewitness saw a blue-gray car in the area where Basom vanished.

Like Skelton, Basom didn't stay missing for long. A few days later, her body was discovered lying beside a road in Ypsilanti. The eighth-grader had been repeatedly slashed across the chest and strangled with an electrical cord. Like Skelton, Basom's cries had been muffled by a piece of cloth shoved down her throat.

After the Basom murder, police managed to find what appeared to be the site of at least one of the slayings—an abandoned farm, just about a half mile from where Fleszar's remains were found. In the barn, officers found a piece of a black electrical cord. The severed ends of the cord matched up with the one the killer used to strangle Dawn Basom.

Police had identified the location where at least one of the murders occurred, but they weren't any closer to identifying the person known in the media as the "Coed Killer."

A few months later, on June 8, 1969, three kids found the body of twenty-three-year-old Alice Kalom. This was the fourth murder in three months. Kalom, a graduate student at the University of Michigan, disappeared after going to a party in Ann Arbor the night before. The killer shot her in the head and then stabbed her numerous times, slashing her neck through to the spine. There was strip of purple cloth from her blouse around her head bandana-style, and she was missing one of her purple high-heel shoes, a detail that would reemerge later when the police zeroed in on a suspect.

The police, feeling pressure from the two communities to stop the Coed Killer, organized a task force with its headquarters in a former Catholic seminary on Washtenaw Avenue. Several police agencies—the Ann Arbor and Ypsilanti police departments, the Washtenaw County Sheriff's Department, and the Michigan State Police—desperately searched for what appeared to be a serial killer.

After the Kalom murder, the public went into panic mode. Frustrated with official efforts, some residents organized their own task force called the "Psychedelic Rangers" and hired renowned psychic Peter Hurkos. The famous medium cited an accident as the source of his psychic abilities. Thirty-eight years earlier, in 1941, Hurkos fell off a ladder, plummeting several stories. He survived the fall and discovered that he had developed new, psychic abilities.

By the late 1960s, Hurkos had worked more than two dozen murder investigations, including the Boston Strangler case, and now the Psychedelic Rangers hoped he could unravel the mystery of the slain coeds. He traveled to Ann Arbor on July 21, 1969.

What specific role Hurkos played in the case remains a point of debate, but he did correctly predict that the killer would murder another victim soon. On July 23, Karen Sue Beineman disappeared.

Investigators combed Ypsilanti for the missing coed. They traced her movements and discovered that she was last seen outside of an Ypsi wig shop, climbing onto a motorcycle with an unidentified young man wearing a striped shirt.

Three days later, on July 26, Beineman's body was found in a wooded ditch on the outskirts of town. She had endured hideous torture before she died. A severe beating left her body covered by bruises. Burns in her mouth and on her chest suggested that her killer had doused her with some caustic agent. During the autopsy, the coroner discovered a piece of cloth in her throat, probably to muffle her cries, and her panties inserted into her vagina. The panties contained a vital piece of forensic evidence—hair clippings—suggesting that Beineman's murder might have taken place somewhere hair was cut.

She was the seventh victim in what people were convinced was a sequence of murders. There were so many similarities among the victims that investigators and media alike believed them to be all connected.

"All girls were brunette Caucasians, and all were murdered in rainy weather," *Time* magazine noted in "Rainy Day Murders," a news item about the Beineman murder published in August 1969. "Six of the seven were strangled, stabbed in the neck or left with something twisted around their necks." There was also some evidence that several of the victims were having their period at the time of their deaths.

Other similarities among the victims seemed to tie them together in a sequence. Five of the seven (excluding Mixer and Kalom) were connected in some way with Eastern Michigan University's campus. All were killed and later dumped in places where they were likely to be found. And all the dumping sites, except Mixer's, occurred in close proximity, forming a geographic pattern.

With the discovery of the Karen Sue Beineman, police had an opportunity to set a trap. Her body was deposited in a heavily forested area. Because of this, police managed to keep their macabre discovery from the media, and so the killer would not know that they had found his latest victim. Since the killer appeared to return to the spots where he dumped his victims, police decided on a ploy to trick him. They removed Beineman's body and replaced it with a mannequin they obtained from a nearby JCPenney. Then they watched the site, waiting for the killer to return.

It rained that night, but despite the weather, they spotted a man walking down Riverside Drive toward the site around midnight. The man walked into the ditch toward the mannequin, but when he discovered plastic instead of flesh, he ran. Officers chased him, but they lost him in the dense woods of the area.

The trap had failed, but police were about to get the lead they needed to stop the killings. When the rain-drenched officers returned from their stakeout of the mannequin, they learned that an EMU campus officer had identified a prime suspect.

After hearing the description of the motorcyclist waiting for Beineman, an EMU campus cop realized that he had seen a man in a striped shirt motoring around EMU that same day. The guy turned out to be John Norman Collins, a twenty-three-year-old EMU student and the same man police questioned after the murder of Joan Schell.

The more the campus cop probed, the more it appeared that Collins was the guy seen with Beineman when she disappeared. Collins was around campus on July 23, a fact established by other women who said that he approached them that day. And eyewitnesses from the wig shop, when shown a photo of Collins, said that he could be the man on the motorcycle, but they couldn't be sure until they saw him in person. It appeared that the first mistake the young coed said she made—buying a wig—might have unveiled her killer.

Collins became the chief suspect. Police watched his every move. They questioned him and asked him to take a polygraph test. At first Collins agreed to the lie-detector test, but then later he changed his mind and refused. Despite a mass of circumstantial evidence, police didn't have a linchpin tying Collins to Karen Sue Beineman. Not yet.

The break in the case came from a source no one expected. A Michigan State Police trooper named David Leik returned to his Ypsilanti residence after a two-week vacation and discovered something strange in his basement: a large swath of black paint, as if his house sitter—his nephew, John Norman Collins—had painted over something.

When he returned to work, Leik learned that Collins was the chief suspect in the Beineman murder. Suddenly, the black swath of paint began to take on sinister overtones, like Collins had tried to cover up something. Leik found what appeared to be bloodstains on the floor underneath the paint. He notified authorities, and a team was sent to comb the residence for clues.

The red stains came from varnish, not blood, but investigators did find spots of blood and hair clippings on the basement floor. The presence of the hair clippings wasn't odd—Leik's wife cut their children's hair in the basement. But the clippings matched those found on Karen Sue Beineman's panties, and the spots of blood turned out to be human. The hair clippings linked Beineman to Leik's basement and to John Norman Collins.

It was the first physical evidence tying Collins to any of the slain coeds, but it would not be the last. The closer detectives looked at Collins during their investigation of the Beineman case, the more strings they found tying him to other victims.

A friend of Collins, Arnie Davis, placed Collins with a woman matching Joan Schell's description the night she disappeared. Davis told police that he was with Collins when Collins met Schell, but Collins and Schell eventually went off together. Collins was apparently going to give the coed a lift to Ann Arbor. He returned a few hours later, alone and disgusted that he and Schell didn't have sex.

Davis also told police that Collins was with a woman matching Alice Kalom's description the night she went missing. According to Davis, Collins and the coed argued behind closed doors, and Kalom ran away with Collins on her heels. Collins returned later, alone. Davis later testified that Collins asked him to hide a knife. Davis gave the knife to investigators, who determined that it was consistent with the weapon used to stab Kalom.

There may have been more evidence linking Collins with the other Michigan victims. Davis described an incident that happened after Collins was questioned about the disappearance of Beineman. Davis watched Collins hurry away carrying a large box partially covered with a blanket. The box contained a purse and other items of clothing including a woman's shoe—a purple pump like the one police found with Alice Kalom. This story led to speculation that the box contained items from the other victims, but police never had the chance to test this theory because Collins disposed of its contents before they searched his property.

If Collins cleaned up evidence before police had a chance to search his stuff, he missed some. Detectives searched his car, an Oldsmobile Cutlass, for evidence he used it in transporting Beineman's body. They found no trace of Beineman in the Olds, but they did find spots of blood matching Kalom's blood type in the front seat. They also found more spots of blood, also matching Kalom's blood type, on a raincoat found in the car. In the pre-DNA days of investigation, this was far from a conclusive physical link, but it was close.

Collins's Oldsmobile also yielded a provocative piece of evidence linking him with an unsolved murder in California. Seventeen-year-old Roxie Phillips disappeared on June 30, 1969, three weeks after Kalom's body was found and about four weeks before Beineman disappeared. Two boys wandering through Pescadero Canyon discovered Phillips's remains in mid-July. She had been strangled. Her body lay in the middle of a poison oak patch and was unclothed except for a red-and-white belt with a very distinctive floral pattern left tied around her neck. Phillips, according to a friend, had met a Michigan student named John, who liked to drive motorcycles and owned a silver Olds. Could John have been John Norman Collins? Collins was in California when Phillips vanished, and that same week he visited a hospital to receive treatment for poison oak.

Across the country in Michigan, police found a slice of a red-and-white cotton belt in the front seat of Collins's car. The cloth, which matched the belt around Phillips's neck, wasn't the only thing tying Collins to Roxie Phillips.

When they went through Collins's closet, Michigan investigators discovered a sweater that was later found to contain twenty-two pubic hairs. The hairs didn't match any of the Michigan victims, so Roxy Phillips's body was exhumed in California to obtain hair samples for comparison. The hairs matched, leading to speculation that

Roxy Phillips's killer carried her over his shoulder before dumping her body in the middle of nowhere. That killer, it now appeared, was John Norman Collins.

It was enough for California authorities, who later convened a grand jury that ultimately indicted Collins for the murder of Roxie Phillips and issued an arrest warrant. But it came too late. Michigan authorities had already collared Collins.

Although investigators had uncovered a trove of circumstantial evidence linking Collins with other Michigan victims, they had a rock-solid case against him for the murder of Karen Sue Beineman. Employees from the wig shop had picked Collins out of a lineup as the man waiting for Beineman. And Arnold Davis told investigators that Collins had attempted to engineer an alibi. Collins wanted Davis to tell police that the two were riding bikes together on July 23 at the time Beineman visited the wig shop.

The most damning evidence against Collins came from Corporal Leik's basement. The spots of blood matched Beineman's blood type, and the hairs on Beineman's panties matched the hairs from the basement floor. Investigators theorized that Collins murdered Beineman in the basement, causing the blood spatter, and then dumped her body in the wooded gully where someone would likely find it. All of the evidence added up to an indictment and charge of premeditated first-degree murder. While prosecutors prepared their case against Collins, the public got a look at the man the press dubbed the Coed Killer.

He was born in Windsor, Ontario, on June 17, 1947. His mother and father split when he was just a toddler. His mother remarried, but this second marriage ended after a year. She relocated to Centerline, Michigan, a suburb of Detroit, where she married again. Collins took the name of his third father figure, who adopted him. John and his stepfather were close, but this marriage lasted only a few years.

Despite the absence of a stable home life during his early years, Collins did well in school. He attended a Roman Catholic school called St. Clements, where he earned a spot on the honor roll and participated in several extracurricular activities. A natural athlete, Collins excelled in sports and became co-captain of the football team.

When he graduated from high school, Collins went to EMU to study education. He joined the ski club and pledged a fraternity. He appeared to be the all-American guy.

But under the exterior of the attractive letterman was a dark side. Collins had a lot of girlfriends, but his dates later described him as angry and aggressive. One former girlfriend said that while on a date, Collins groped her. When she told him that she was having her period, he yelled and stormed off. This incident has led to speculation about the Coed Killer's motive: several of the women were having their periods when they were murdered. Did something about menstruation bother Collins so much that it drove him to murder?

Another woman said that during a date, Collins alluded to being the Coed Killer. If he were the killer, would she be afraid? he asked. And then he mentioned that she could be the Coed Killer's next victim. Was it a macabre joke, or did Collins know something about the co-ed slayings?

According to another female acquaintance, Collins claimed he knew how to commit the ideal murder. To another, he admitted killing a cat when he was a child. Another alleged that Collins raped her while on a date.

He also stole things. He was ejected from the Theta Chi fraternity amid allegations of theft, and the four bikes on which he motored around Ypsilanti and Ann Arbor ran on mostly pilfered parts. His small theft evolved into grand larceny when he stole a trailer, which he took to California in 1969 around the time Roxie Phillips was murdered.

*People v. Collins* began on June 30, 1970, in front of a packed courtroom and an eager press, who reported every detail about the Coed Killer's trial. They had plenty of material. The prosecution paraded witness after witness in front of the jury. Eyewitnesses testified to seeing Collins with Karen Sue Beineman, and forensics experts testified about the physical evidence placing her in Leik's basement.

Collins's lawyers thought about putting the all-American boy on the stand, but during trial prep, Collins couldn't control his temper. So they decided to leave the final decision to Collins's mother. After a short recess, Collins emerged from a conference room with his mother, who appeared shaken. The defense rested and the jury went into deliberations without hearing from the defendant.

The jury returned a verdict of guilty—a decision that would send Collins to prison for the rest of his life. During sentencing, Collins addressed the court, insisting that he never even met Karen Sue Beineman.

Since California authorities had convened a grand jury that indicted Collins, California governor Ronald Reagan requested extradition of Collins in December 1970, but Michigan governor William Milliken denied the request. Collins was in a Michigan prison and facing a lengthy appeals process, so California authorities decided to file the case, which would be an insurance policy should an appeals court overturn Collins's conviction.

It didn't. Collins lost all of his appeals.

Although he rarely speaks publicly, Collins has not changed his story since the trial. In 1988, he spoke on a talk show and reiterated his claim that he never met the victim for whose murder he was serving a life sentence. He alleged that the police, desperate for an arrest, framed him. When asked about the positive identification made by the employees of the Ypsilanti wig shop, Collins explained that the two women couldn't agree about the hair style of the man outside on the motorcycle, which according to Collins calls into question the accuracy of their identification. The media, he added, had unfairly labeled him a serial killer.

The murders of Fleszar, Schell, Skelton, Basom, and Kalom remain officially unsolved and lack the closure of a court conviction. Despite this fact, the court of public opinion has convicted a single, Bundyesque serial killer for the entire string, and when

Collins was arrested, he gave the public a face to go with the nickname Coed Killer. Even though a body of tantalizing clues and circumstantial evidence link John Norman Collins to the other co-ed slayings, unless there is a deathbed confession or new DNA evidence, the extent of Collins' crimes, it appears, will forever remain speculative. But there has been official closure on another one of the seven co-ed cases. In 2005, a jury convicted Gary Leiterman of murdering Jane Mixer, who some believed to be the third in the supposed sequence of slayings.

Of the seven murders, Mixer's differed from the others in several key regards, and even members of the official investigation questioned whether her death was linked with the others. She was clothed, not nude, shot in the head with a .22, and deposited in a cemetery not close to the other dumping sites. And her killer didn't sexually molest her.

Thirty-five years after Mixer's murder, a DNA test of material found on Mixer's pantyhose linked her with Leiterman, who lived about twenty miles away from Ann Arbor in 1969. A prior fraud conviction placed Leiterman's DNA in the FBI database, so when investigators discovered DNA evidence on Mixer's pantyhose and ran it through the system for a match, Leiterman's name popped up. The DNA evidence suggested that Leiterman had contact with Mixer around the time she disappeared.

But there was a problem. An analysis of a blood spot supposedly found on Mixer's left hand revealed the DNA of another man—John Ruelas—who was convicted of murdering his mother in 2002. The discovery of Ruelas's DNA on Mixer's hand was an odd discovery, because Ruelas was just four years old when Mixer was murdered. It also raised an evidentiary issue in the case against Leiterman. Evidence from the Ruelas case was processed at the same time and at the same lab as evidence from the Mixer case, raising suspicions about contaminated samples.

So at Leiterman's trial, which took place in July 2005, DNA became the focal point. The trial captured national headlines as experts battled experts about the handling of evidence and the validity of DNA analysis. In some ways, DNA analysis was put on trial alongside sixty-two-year-old Gary Leiterman.

The DNA match wasn't the prosecution's only evidence. Prosecutors also introduced the telephone book found on the university's law campus in 1969 with the handwritten notations "Muskegeon" and "Mixer." An expert matched the handwriting with Leiterman's.

Leiterman also once owned a .22, and a ballistics expert testified that the bullet fragments dug out of Mixer's head were similar to bullets found at Leiterman's residence, although the expert also testified that they were the most common type of .22 bullet sold.

After hearing from dozens of witnesses, the jury convicted Leiterman of premeditated, first-degree murder. His first appeal, based mostly on the DNA evidence presented in court, failed in the Michigan Court of Appeals in 2007.

John Norman Collins tried to escape his prison sentence in a few different ways. He tried to tunnel his way out of Marquette State Prison in 1979 along with several other inmates. The erstwhile escapees managed to dig a nineteen-foot-long tunnel, but with twenty-five feet to go, they were caught less than halfway to daylight.

After the failed escape attempt, Collins was confined to a secure cell block, where he spent twenty-three hours a day in his cell. While there, he had plenty of time to hatch a more subtle plan to escape his life sentence.

In 1982, Collins attempted to gain extradition to his native Canada. Under Canadian law, Collins would have been up for parole in 1985. Once again, he failed.

He currently resides in Marquette State Prison in the Upper Peninsula—as far away from Ypsilanti as possible.

# CHAPTER 9

# Riddle is My Middle Name: The Disappearance of Jimmy Hoffa

✳ ✳ ✳

**Jimmy Hoffa stepped** out of a Detroit-area restaurant in 1975 and stepped into history as one of America's most elusive missing persons. Since his disappearance, several convicted killers have confessed to playing a role in Hoffa's killing. The many, often conflicting, stories of the murder and disposal of Hoffa's body have led authorities to dismantle a barn, dig below a swimming pool, and pull up the flooring of a house. Despite these and many other efforts, investigators have not yet found his body. Among the tangled mess of lies, investigators did find a tantalizing clue about Hoffa's possible fate—a single strand of hair.

✳ ✳ ✳

The day he disappeared, Hoffa thought he had a meeting with two powerful underworld figures: Anthony "Tony Jack" Giacalone and Anthony "Tony Pro" Provenzano. As a reminder, Hoffa left a note taped to a lampshade in his home office: "T G" at the "Fox Rest" (the Machus Red Fox Restaurant) at 2 P.M. on July 30, 1975.

Hoffa waited at the Red Fox, an upscale eatery in the affluent Detroit suburb of Bloomfield Township, but no one showed up. Disgusted, he left the restaurant and walked to a nearby hardware store to call his wife from a pay phone. "I wonder where the hell Tony is. I'm waiting for him," he said.

He couldn't believe the two men would have the nerve to miss the meeting. It took months to arrange. The relationship between Hoffa and New Jersey Teamster leader Tony Pro had deteriorated into a feud over the last few years, and Tony Jack had tried several times to bring the two men together to settle their differences. Each time, Hoffa refused. He called Tony Pro a "bum" and told Tony Jack that he would never meet Tony Pro.

But by midsummer 1975, he had agreed to a meeting. The talk, he believed, would be about his desire to rejoin the Teamster leadership. He had been bounced from the Teamsters when he was convicted for jury tampering in 1967. Now, he wanted to reclaim his spot at the top of the hierarchy. Tony Jack, Tony Pro, and others wanted him to stay away from Teamster politics, and they may have been worried about what Hoffa would do to achieve his goal. He knew a great deal of information about illegal activity inside the Teamster organization—information he could use as leverage to recapture his former position as Teamster president.

Angry and puzzled, Hoffa walked back to the Red Fox. Shortly after, an eyewitness allegedly saw Hoffa, along with three other men, in the backseat of a maroon Mercury sedan that was leaving the parking lot of the Red Fox. Hoffa hasn't been seen since.

The next day, the search for Hoffa began. Local authorities and the FBI immediately launched investigations. Hoffa's car, a 1974 Pontiac Grand Ville, was still parked at the Red Fox but they found nothing unusual in it. Hoffa, it appeared, left the parking lot in another car, and perhaps it would be the key to finding him.

Detectives believed that Hoffa wouldn't have left the Red Fox unless it was with someone he trusted, and that short list included Teamster Charles L. "Chuckie" O'Brien. On July 30, O'Brien—a longtime friend of the Hoffa family and a very close associate of Tony Jack—was in the area driving a 1975 maroon Mercury he borrowed from Tony Jack's son Joseph. O'Brien told investigators that he had used the car to run an errand but said he did not go to the Red Fox or see Hoffa that day. The FBI decided to search the vehicle for clues. On August 9, agents seized and examined the Mercury.

Inside the car, federal agents found twenty-six latent fingerprints. Ten of the prints came from O'Brien, one came from an FBI agent who seized the car, and the other fifteen were unidentified. Three special agents—trained German shepherds—also went through the vehicle. All three dogs sniffed out Hoffa's scent in the back rear seat, and one dog detected Hoffa's scent in the car's trunk.

But investigators found the real prize in the backseat: a single strand of brown hair that matched the color and texture of Hoffa's. In 2001, a DNA comparison of this hair and one taken from Hoffa's hairbrush matched. The hair, although it didn't prove when or even if Hoffa was in the car, was a tantalizing clue—but where did the rest of Hoffa go, and who were the other three men allegedly seen with him at the Red Fox?

In June 2006, the *Detroit Free Press* published the "Hoffex Memo," the FBI's 1976 report detailing its investigation of the Hoffa disappearance. The memo presents a shady lineup of characters that investigators believed knew about or played a direct role in a conspiracy to murder Hoffa.

The two men Hoffa believed he was going to meet—Tony Jack and Tony Pro—topped the list of suspects. Both Tony Jack and Tony Pro told investigators that they knew of no such meeting with Hoffa. And both men had alibis for their whereabouts on the afternoon of July 30. Tony Pro was at a card game in New Jersey, and Tony Jack spent the afternoon at the Southfield Athletic Club. Tony Jack usually stayed out of the public eye, but the afternoon Hoffa disappeared, he seemed to make it a point to be seen. Several witnesses verified his presence at the health club during the time frame when Hoffa vanished.

Chuckie O'Brien admitted that he drove Joseph Giacalone's maroon Mercury on July 30, but he insisted that Hoffa was never in the car and denied any involvement in Hoffa's disappearance. He had always been intensely loyal to the man who helped raise him. The Hoffa family took in O'Brien at age three when his father died. O'Brien always thought of Hoffa as a father.

But O'Brien also had close ties with Tony Jack, whom he called "Uncle Tony." Tony Jack dated O'Brien's mother, and O'Brien may have had a disagreement with Hoffa about union leadership. Frank Fitzsimmons, who replaced Hoffa as Teamster president when Hoffa went to prison, gave O'Brien a cushy job with a generous salary, leading investigators to wonder if O'Brien had become an ally of Fitzsimmons, Hoffa's rival for power.

O'Brien also had an alibi. During interviews with the FBI, O'Brien sketched out an elaborate story of his whereabouts on July 30. O'Brien told detectives that he used the maroon Mercury to deliver a coho salmon to the home of local union leader Robert Holmes Sr. When he left the Holmes residence, he noticed that the fish had leaked blood onto the car's upholstery, so he took the Mercury to a car wash. Federal investigators checked and rechecked O'Brien's story and found numerous inconsistencies, but they found no direct, concrete evidence linking him to Hoffa's disappearance.

Despite his alibi and his insistence that he had nothing to do with it, Chuckie O'Brien's name would resurface in several Hoffa disappearance theories as one of the three men allegedly seen with Hoffa in the Red Fox parking lot. The usually cautious Hoffa trusted O'Brien enough to leave the restaurant with him, fueling speculation that the killers used O'Brien as an unwitting accomplice in a plot to assassinate the former labor leader.

Federal investigators followed a line that conspirators used a fictitious meeting with Tony Pro to lure Hoffa to the Red Fox, where he was to be picked up and taken to the rendezvous. According to the FBI's theory, the conspirators would have used someone familiar with Hoffa—someone who probably didn't know about the murder plot—to lull him into a false sense of security. With a trusted friend at his side, Hoffa wouldn't think twice about leaving the restaurant in someone else's car. So Hoffa climbed into the Mercury and was taken for a ride. But the meeting isn't a peace conference with the powerful East Coast Teamster: it's an execution engineered by high-ranking mobsters.

If the FBI's theory was correct and Hoffa was "taken for ride," who were the executioners? The Hoffex Memo's short list of prime suspects included Salvatore "Sally Bugs" Briguglio and Frank "The Irishman" Sheeran, both known associates of mobsters.

By the time of Hoffa's disappearance, Briguglio had acquired a reputation as Tony Pro's muscle. He allegedly played a role in the 1961 disappearance of a Teamster treasurer in circumstances that mirrored the Hoffa case. An eyewitness picked him out of a lineup as a man she saw sitting in a maroon car at the Red Fox.

Frank Sheeran was a Teamster official from Delaware and right-hand man to Pennsylvania mob boss Russell Bufalino. Sheeran was a good friend of Hoffa, and he was known to be in Detroit on July 30. Hoffa trusted him enough to get into a car with him and may even have believed that Sheeran would protect him at the meeting. But the FBI could not get Sheeran to talk. He pled the fifth in front of a grand jury.

The FBI's list of suspects included others, but few wanted to talk about Hoffa, July 30, corruption in the Teamsters, or the mafia. Their silence left investigators with plenty of speculation but no concrete evidence, no indictments, and no Jimmy Hoffa.

If Hoffa was murdered on the afternoon of July 30, 1975, it was the end of a story that began sixty years earlier in the Wild West atmosphere of a Midwestern boomtown where the future labor leader James Riddle Hoffa was born.

In the late 1800s, coal fueled much of America, and Clay County in southwestern Indiana had plenty of it. In 1871, surveyors discovered massive coal deposits in the area around the tiny town of Brazil. The coal industry offered stable, if treacherous, employment. Even though mining was risky business, the promise of steady work lured people to the area.

John Cleveland Hoffa, his young wife Viola, and their infant daughter Jenetta joined the migration to Clay County, where John Hoffa went to work as a drill operator for an independent coal prospector. The young family settled in an area of Brazil populated by coal miners. A few years later, Viola gave birth to William Henry, and on Valentine's Day 1913, James Riddle was born.

The setting of Jimmy Hoffa's childhood may have played a pivotal role in his future as a labor activist. Poor working conditions had spawned a growing socialist movement in the United States, but in southwestern Indiana, a few companies controlled the coal mining industry, and people owed their souls to the company stores.

Despite the boom, coal-mining communities suffered many hardships and tragedies brought on by the dangerous conditions in the mines. Accidents, such as shaft cave-ins, fires, and dust explosions, killed miners every year. Others died from pneumonia or illnesses caused by inhaling coal dust, such as black lung disease, leaving their wives and children without a means to survive. Some young widows, with no other way to support their families, remarried. Others joined the oldest profession and became prostitutes.

They didn't have to look far for employers. Like other boomtowns, Brazil offered its hardworking miners an array of diversions and hosted a red light subculture of brothels, casinos, and saloons. The center of the action—Meridian Street—became the scene of brawling, theft, and murder, earning it the nickname "Bloody Row." Young Jimmy Hoffa lived just a few blocks away.

While Jimmy played with his siblings just a stone's throw from the city's capital of vice, John Hoffa explored the area around Brazil, searching for the rich coal deposits that gave rise to this mixture of people. In 1920, tragedy struck the Hoffas: John came home from work sick. He died a week later, likely another victim of black lung.

Viola now found herself in the difficult position of supporting a family of five. The tenacious Hoffa matriarch rolled up her sleeves and went to work doing laundry and cleaning houses, but these jobs did not generate enough income to support her four children. And by 1920, Brazil was no longer a boomtown. It was just a town— several of its chief mines had been exhausted.

So the Hoffas moved to Clinton, a thriving coal-mining community where Viola had relatives. Determined to keep her family afloat, she opened Hoffa Home Laundry. True to its name, the enterprise involved the entire Hoffa clan. Jimmy and his brother Billy collected the soot-covered clothes of the miners and delivered them to their mother, who scrubbed clean the town's dirty laundry.

Like Brazil, Clinton had a real wild side, and young Jimmy had a front-row seat. Strikes by disgruntled workers often led to brawls among miners, cops, and scabs brought in to cross the picket lines. The birth of Prohibition gave rise to bootlegging, which led to even more mayhem. Raids resulted in shootouts between police and the Italian mobs that controlled the illegal trade of booze.

Clinton's glory, however, was short-lived. The rise of the automobile, which ran on gasoline, not coal, indirectly led to the atrophy of Clinton and the other coal-mining towns. So once again, in 1924, the Hoffas followed the crowd north to the nation's new boomtown, Detroit. Jimmy was eleven.

Thanks to Henry Ford's Model-T and the assembly line, Detroit's population swelled to over a million residents in the 1920s. They came from all over the country for jobs in the automotive plants and supporting industries. The Motor City was born.

Viola began her life in Detroit the way she ended it in Clinton— doing the city's laundry. But not for long. The auto industry did offer a few jobs to women, and Viola went to work for General Motors. As a woman in a male-dominated field, however, she didn't make enough money to support the family. So while still a preteen, Jimmy went to work after school part time for a local grocery store.

After the ninth grade, Hoffa dropped out of school so he could go to work full time. Hoffa's first full-time job was for a dry goods store as a stock boy earning $2 a day. Wages were low and conditions poor, so the workers made several attempts to organize themselves into a union. Eventually, with street sense and a keen wit for organization, Hoffa made his way to the top of these efforts.

Hoffa's legend as a union activist was born in 1930 when he organized a strike against supermarket giant Kroger. The strike took place at the loading docks just as a shipment of fresh strawberries arrived. Hoffa's timing was perfect. Lengthy negotiations meant spoiled fruit, so the owners quickly made a deal that would keep the strawberries from spoiling. The "Strawberry Boys" negotiated a new contract within an hour, and Hoffa chalked up his first big win against management.

After their victory over Kroger, Hoffa and his Strawberry Boys joined Teamsters Local 674, a local branch of the labor giant known as the International Brotherhood of Teamsters. The crafty Hoffa transformed the organization from a small band of forty to a large group of five thousand with a bankroll of $50,000. Hoffa had become a major player in organized labor.

In 1941, Hoffa's reputation took a sinister turn when he became involved with organized crime. The Teamsters were entangled in a feud with another labor union, the Congress of Industrial Organizations (CIO). To win this turf war, Hoffa turned to Detroit-based crime bosses, who ran the CIO out of town. Hoffa won the feud, but he became forever linked with organized crime.

Over the next few years, Hoffa continued to rattle management with his labor activities, making many enemies along the way. Relations between management and workers were often contentious, with company employees and police tangling with workers. And in the middle of the melee was Jimmy Hoffa. His car was bombed, and in one day alone, he was arrested eighteen times.

But try as they might, Hoffa's enemies just couldn't get rid of the plucky union leader. In 1952, Hoffa became vice president of the Teamsters. In that position, Hoffa spearheaded the first national freight-hauling agreement that brought all U.S. truck drivers together. Then in 1957, amid rumors of fraud, Hoffa won a controversial election and became the Teamsters' president.

By the late 1960s, mobsters had infiltrated the Teamsters at all levels. Several underworld figures assumed prominent positions in the union, and the rumors flew about ties that bound the Teamsters to organized crime. "Paper locals" were developed as fronts for various illegal activities, including loan sharking, racketeering, extortion, drug trafficking, and bribery.

But the real treasure chest was the Central States Pension Fund—the massive retirement fund for the Teamster organization. Under Hoffa's leadership, the Teamsters' pension fund bankrolled the business of some shady characters like Morris "Moe" Dalitz, a former associate of Detroit's Purple Gang. During Prohibition, Dalitz used his father's laundry trucks to ferry alcohol into Detroit from Canada. He eventually channeled his illegal profits into legal ventures, which included gaming in Nevada. With low-interest loans from the Central States Pension Fund, he built Las Vegas's Desert Inn and acquired control of the Stardust and the Fremont casinos.

Dalitz wasn't the only one cashing in. According to some sources, much of the Las Vegas strip owes its existence to low-interest loans from the Teamsters pension fund.

Despite appearances, however, organized crime didn't control Hoffa. They may have relied on him for illicit loans, but they didn't tell the tenacious union leader what to do. No one did.

"I may have faults," Hoffa once said, "but being wrong ain't one of them." And he made sure that he wasn't. Hoffa knew how to get his way, either over the table or under it.

One of his under-the-table dealings put Hoffa in front of a jury for allegedly taking a million-dollar bribe to ensure labor peace at a particular company. The jury acquitted Hoffa, but on the final day of the trial, he faced another charge for attempting to bribe one of the jurors. In 1964, he was sentenced to eight years, but subsequent convictions (one for mail fraud and another for misuse of union pension funds) compounded his sentence to thirteen years.

At the Federal Penitentiary at Lewisburg, Pennsylvania, Hoffa did time with Anthony Provenzano, or Tony Pro. The son of Sicilian immigrants, he became a truck driver at eighteen and worked his way up the Teamster ranks. Like Hoffa, Tony Pro was tenacious and knew how to get his way.

Tony Pro was also a member of New Jersey's La Costa Nostra and ran Teamsters Local 560 in Union City, New Jersey, one of the most corrupt branches in the country. The 560 gave him easy access to union funds that he could use to bankroll various illegal activities. He was a very dangerous man to cross. And that is just what Hoffa did. While they were at Lewisburg together, something led to a rift between Hoffa and Tony Pro. The possible disagreement may have come when Tony Pro asked Hoffa to help him recover a pension fund and Hoffa refused. Or the rift may have formed when Tony Pro learned that Hoffa planned to wrest control of the Teamsters from Tony Pro's ally Frank Fitzsimmons. Hoffa told one Teamster acquaintance that Tony Pro threatened to murder him if he ran for the Teamster presidency.

Hoffa had spent five years in prison when President Richard Nixon commuted his sentence in 1971. As a condition of his pardon, Hoffa could not participate in the Teamsters until 1980. When he was released from prison, however, he expected that this ban would be lifted, and he planned to retake control of the Teamsters.

Hoffa's reentry into the Teamsters threatened the mobsters who benefited from the corrupt system that flourished under Fitzsimmons. Hoffa once said, "I don't intend to have the impression left that I am controlled by gangsters. I am not controlled by them."

Frank Fitzsimmons, on the other hand, was much easier to control. He delegated a great deal of power to local Teamster officials. So under Fitzsimmons's leadership, corrupt Teamster officials gave mobsters free reign in the union.

Fitzsimmons was also the perfect front man. Well liked by Nixon, Fitzsimmons didn't have Hoffa's criminal record. Federal authorities were less likely to watch Teamster activity with Fitzsimmons in control, and corrupt Teamsters could carry on with their rackets. Hoffa was a threat to this group, which included Tony Pro.

And Tony Pro's problems tended to vanish. One such disappearance linked to Tony Pro bears a striking resemblance to the Hoffa case. In 1961, the 560's secretary-treasurer, Anthony Castellito, traveled to upstate New York to meet with Salvatore "Sally Bugs" Briguglio. While Tony Pro was enjoying the Florida sun, Briguglio and a group of co-conspirators allegedly murdered Castellito and ran the secretary's body through a wood chipper. Tony Pro then appointed Briguglio to Castellito's position.

But then Briguglio may have become a problem. In 1976, Briguglio and Tony Pro were indicted for Castellito's murder. Some speculate that Briguglio was about to rat on his former employer and was negotiating with the feds in exchange for his testimony. Briguglio never had the chance. He was gunned down in New York on Little Italy's Mulberry Street before he could turn state's evidence. Even though Briguglio couldn't testify, a few months later, a jury found Tony Pro guilty of Castellito's murder.

Was Jimmy Hoffa another Castellito? One FBI source told investigators that Tony Pro had attempted on two previous occasions to lure Hoffa to a meeting with the purpose of having Hoffa murdered. During its investigation, the FBI found an informant named Ralph Picardo, a Teamster and former driver for Tony Pro, who claimed to know all about what happened to Hoffa. If Picardo's story is accurate, then Hoffa's demise was a mirror image of Castellito's.

According to Picardo, shortly after Hoffa's disappearance, a few business associates came to visit him in a New Jersey prison where he was doing time for murder. One of these men told him about Hoffa's execution.

Hoffa was chauffeured from the Red Fox to a nearby house where he believed he would meet with Tony Jack and Tony Pro. But instead, Salvatore Briguglio, Frank Sheeran, and two other men waited for Hoffa, who was murdered when he entered the house. His body was then taken to New Jersey. According to Picardo, Russell Bufalino ordered the hit and gave the contract to Tony Pro, who arranged the setup. Bufalino was in Detroit on July 30; some speculate that he may have even witnessed the execution.

Picardo's story, which many investigators believe to be the most credible, was just the first of many Hoffa execution tales. In the thirty-five years since Hoffa vanished, a motley crew of suspicious characters—most of them dying killers or felons attempting to swap information with authorities—have confessed to playing some role in the crime or cover-up or both. The stories, which range from the possible to the incredible, have sent investigators all over the place with picks, shovels, and ground-penetrating radar looking for some trace of Jimmy Hoffa. The names and places change from story to story, but one common theme unites them: The mob murdered Hoffa to keep him away from the Teamsters.

In 1989, a Hoffa assassination tale sent investigators to Giants Stadium in East Rutherford, New Jersey. Convicted murderer and mob assassin Donald Frankos claimed to be one of the triggermen in Hoffa's murder. Frankos's criminal career is documented in *Contract Killer: The Explosive Story of the Mafia's Most Notorious Hitman*, a book written with Frankos's cooperation by authors William Hoffman and Lake Headley.

Frankos, also known as "Tony the Greek," appears to have had the perfect alibi: When Hoffa disappeared, Frankos was serving a prison sentence for murder. The alibi, according to Frankos, was actually the ideal cover. He was let out of prison on temporary furloughs that he used to complete murder contracts.

One of these contracts was for Jimmy Hoffa. According to Frankos, Hoffa was taken to a Detroit house where a hit team waited. Frankos and another man shot Hoffa, dismembered his corpse, and kept the pieces in a basement freezer until they could decide what to do with them. The remains were sealed in an oil drum and buried beneath the turf of Giants Stadium. In 2004, a crew from the television show *Myth Busters* searched Giants Stadium using ground-penetrating radar, but they didn't find Hoffa.

In 2003, authorities searched a property in Bay City, Michigan, about one hundred miles north of Detroit, for clues about the labor leader's fate. They were acting on a tip by another murderer who claimed to know what happened to Hoffa. Richard Powell, convicted of murdering his landlady in 1982, said he played a part in Hoffa's disappearance. Powell said that he worked alongside mobsters in an auto theft ring in the 1970s. He was ordered to transport a body, which was wrapped in a rug, from Detroit to northern Michigan. Someone else, he said, disposed of Hoffa's corpse.

No one took Powell's story seriously until he led police to the body of another missing person. In 2003, Powell said that he had buried a body in a crawl space under the house he occupied in the 1970s. Investigators found Robert Woods, a Bay City man missing since the 1970s, just where Powell said they would. If Powell told the truth about Woods, maybe he was telling the truth about Hoffa.

So when Powell told investigators that they could find, buried in the backyard, a briefcase containing evidence of Hoffa's murder, they listened. According to Powell, the briefcase contained a syringe used to tranquilize or possibly poison Hoffa, a pack of playing cards, and handwritten notes of the conspirators. If the briefcase existed, forensic scientists could possibly lift fingerprints from the syringe and the cards to identify those involved. But after a six-hour search that included unearthing a swimming pool, investigators left the property empty-handed.

Of all the Hoffa admissions, only one comes from a man on the FBI's original list of suspects: Frank Sheeran. Like many of the other suspects on the list, Sheeran wouldn't talk to investigators in 1975. Almost thirty years after Hoffa disappeared, he had a change of heart.

Dying of cancer, Sheeran decided to clear his conscience. He told several conflicting versions of his role in Hoffa's murder. At first, he said that someone else shot Hoffa, but then he changed his story. He admitted to author Charles Brandt that he was the triggerman in Hoffa's execution. Brandt wrote a book called *I Heard You Paint Houses*, detailing the hit man's career, including Sheeran's account of Hoffa's disappearance.

Sheeran had served in World War II. When he returned from Europe, he became a truck driver and a Teamster. Eventually, Sheeran met Hoffa, and the two became close friends.

According to Sheeran, the first thing Hoffa said to him was "I heard you paint houses," mob slang for contract killing (shots to the head result in a blood spray that "paints" the walls red). Like many other Teamsters of the time, Sheeran rubbed elbows with mobsters and sometimes moonlighted as a mob assassin and painted walls—twenty-five to thirty in total. Many of these hits were for Russell Bufalino. By his own admission, Sheeran painted the walls of a suburban house not far from the Red Fox restaurant with the blood of his friend Jimmy Hoffa. Bufalino, Sheeran said, ordered the hit because Hoffa had become a liability to the mob's operations with the Teamsters, especially its business with Las Vegas casinos.

Sheeran didn't want to whack his friend, but he characterized Bufalino as a ruthless character who didn't take no for an answer. People who did say no to Bufalino "went to Australia," mob slang for murder. Besides, Sheeran was the perfect choice for the job. Hoffa trusted him enough to leave the Red Fox in his company and probably thought of Sheeran as his protection. Sheeran told Hoffa that he would meet him at the Red Fox with "his little brother"—a gun—and ride shotgun during the meeting with Tony Pro. Little did Hoffa know that his meeting would be with Sheeran's "little brother" and not the New Jersey Teamster.

Sheeran said he arrived at the Red Fox at 2:40 P.M. with Briguglio and Chuckie O'Brien, who knew nothing about the murder plot. With O'Brien driving and Hoffa in the backseat, the foursome traveled eight miles to a house on Beaverland Street.

When they arrived at the house, Sheeran said, O'Brien and Briguglio left in the Mercury while Sheeran followed Hoffa into the house. Once inside, Hoffa realized what was about to happen and started for the door, but he didn't make it. Sheeran shot him twice in the back of the head, dropped the gun, and left. The mob had stationed two men inside the house to clean up the scene and dispose of the body. The cleaners took Hoffa's body to a nearby mortuary, where it was cremated, and sanitized the crime scene.

After Sheeran's story went public, investigators searched the house and took samples of blood from the floorboards. But the blood did not match Hoffa's. Sheeran died in 2003.

The lineup of possible Hoffa assassins became a little more crowded when Richard "the Ice Man" Kuklinski confessed. The Ice Man said he worked for several mafia families and claimed to have murdered more than a hundred men during his career (authorities doubt Kuklinski iced that many people). Kuklinski had no problem talking about his criminal career and seemed to revel in fantastic stories of murders he said he committed (he once said he murdered a mark with an exploding, remote-controlled car). One of his many victims, he told Philip Carlo, author of *The Ice Man: Confessions of a Mafia Contract Killer*, was Jimmy Hoffa.

According to the Ice Man, he and three others met Hoffa at the Red Fox. When Hoffa stepped into their car, Kuklinski stabbed Hoffa in the back of the head. He took the body to New Jersey, burned it, and sealed it in a steel drum. The steel drum was placed in the trunk of a car that was crushed and sold as scrap metal to a Japanese car company. Hoffa, Kuklinski said, became part of a car. The Ice Man died of natural causes in 2006 while serving a life sentence for murder in an unrelated case.

Just two months after the Ice Man died, investigators followed a tip to a Milford farm once owned by Teamster Rolland McMaster, one of the FBI's original suspects. Authorities called it the most promising lead they received in the case in thirty years. The tip came from Donovan Wells, a convicted drug trafficker in federal prison. Wells told detectives that when he lived on the farm, local mafia leaders used the barn as a meeting place. In 1975, Wells saw a backhoe arrive and watched men bury a cylindrical object under the barn. According to Wells, McMaster told him that the cylindrical object contained Hoffa. McMaster denied the allegation.

McMaster, like the other suspects on the FBI's list, did not want Hoffa to return as Teamster president. Although not one shred of direct evidence links McMaster to Hoffa's disappearance (he was in Gary, Indiana, on July 30), the FBI considered him a suspect because of his history as a union enforcer and his ties with Detroit Teamsters Local 299. Several instances of violence occurred at the farm by known McMaster associates, and McMaster had a reputation as a bully with mob connections. Did Hoffa's body lie hidden somewhere in the dirt of McMaster's horse farm?

To answer this question, a team of agents, anthropologists, and archaeologists began a massive excavation in May 2006. Investigators cratered the farm looking for the grave. They even dismantled the barn. But they didn't find Hoffa. If McMaster knew anything, he took it with him; he died in 2007.

Most of the goodfellas and corrupt Teamsters the FBI suspected of writing Hoffa's vanishing act are taking the dead man's fifth. Tony Pro died of heart failure while doing time for Castellito's murder. Tony Jack Giacalone did ten years for tax evasion and faced racketeering charges, but died before the trial. Russell Bufalino, the mob boss that both Picardo and Sheeran fingered as ordering Hoffa's execution, did separate stints in prison for extortion and attempted murder. He died in 1994. If any of these men knew something about Hoffa's fate, they won't be talking.

Chuckie O'Brien, who all along has adamantly denied any involvement with Hoffa's disappearance, moved to Florida when Frank Fitzsimmons gave him a role in the Teamsters there. In 1979, he did a ten-month stint in prison for a labor law violation. In 1990, he was ejected from the Teamsters for his alleged ties to organized crime.

The search for Jimmy Hoffa continues, but maybe there isn't anything to find. In Sheerhan's story, Hoffa is cremated. In the Ice Man's account, he becomes part of a bumper. According to another story, Hoffa's body was melted in a container of boiling zinc. And in another, he was run through a tire shredder. Perhaps Hoffa will never be found because he's gone with the wind. All that physically remains of the labor leader is a single hair that has led to endless speculation about the who, what, and where of America's most infamous missing person.

# CHAPTER 10

# In (and Out of) Hot Water: The Criminal Career of Coral Watts

After the "Sunday Morning Slasher" was finally caught red-handed in Texas, a Michigan detective interviewed the serial killer about some of his crimes in the Great Lakes State. Curious about the extent of Coral Watts's criminal career, the detective asked if he had enough fingers and toes to count all of his victims.

Watts looked around the room and counted five, including himself. "There's not enough fingers and toes in this room," he said. Five people, a hundred digits—a number that would make Coral Watts one of America's most prolific serial killers.

"The Sunday Morning Slasher"—Carl Eugene Watts—was born on November 7, 1953, in Killeen, Texas. His father Richard, a private in the U.S. Army, was stationed at Fort Hood, but just days after Carl's birth, the family moved back to their hometown of Coalwood, West Virginia.

When Carl was two years old, his parents divorced. His mother Dorothy took the two children to Inkster, Michigan, where she got a job as an art teacher. Although he sometimes struggled with academics, Carl was a fine student and earned good grades.

During the next few years, the family made frequent visits to Coalwood. Carl loved to hunt small game with his grandfather and play with his cousins. It was during one of these visits that Watts acquired his new name. His cousins spoke with rural drawl and pronounced Carl as "Coral." Watts liked the nickname and re-christened himself Coral Watts.

At eight, Coral contracted polio and viral meningitis, which caused a terrific fever, and he spent several months in an area hospital battling both diseases. He received frequent spinal taps and began to complain about lapses in memory. He missed months of school and fell behind his peers.

A shy boy, Coral was quiet and reserved, but he was an outstanding athlete. He excelled on both the baseball diamond and the football field, and as a teenager, he won a middleweight Golden Gloves title. But he continued to lag behind in school. At age fifteen, Coral was reading at a fourth-grade level.

As a kid, Coral could be temperamental but showed no signs of the violent behavior that would later make him infamous. That changed in 1969 when the fifteen-year-old Watts attacked a twenty-six-year-old woman without provocation. While delivering newspapers, he attacked the woman, punched her several times, and then walked away from the scene. A few days later, police arrested Watts. When asked about the crime, Watts said that he "just felt like beating someone."

Watts checked into a center for forensic psychiatry in Detroit where doctors studied the enigmatic teen. It became clear that he felt animosity and even hostility toward women. He expressed no remorse for the random attack and said that he often dreamt of beating and killing women. A few years later, these dreams would become Coral's reality.

In high school, Coral continued to box and play football, but he also became antisocial and experimented with drugs. In 1973, despite these issues, Watts managed to graduate at the age of nineteen. He went to Lane College in Tennessee on a football scholarship, but he didn't stay long. After only three months, his football career was cut short by a knee injury. He returned to Detroit to live with his mother and took a job as a mechanic.

In 1974, twenty-year-old Watts went back to college at Western Michigan University in Kalamazoo. While he was studying at WMU, a series of crimes against women terrorized coeds.

On the morning of October 25, Lenore Knizacky answered a knock on her apartment door. A young black man asked to see Charles. Knizacky told the man that she didn't know a Charles but suggested that he check neighboring apartments. A little while later, the man returned.

Knizacky asked the stranger if he wanted to leave a note. When she unchained the door and turned, he jumped on her and forced her to the floor. He choked her until she lost consciousness, and then he walked away from the apartment. Knizacky survived the attack, but her assailant's next victim wouldn't be so lucky.

On the morning of October 30, 1974 the mysterious friend of "Charles" rapped on the door of Apartment 350 in the Stadium Drive complex. Nineteen-year-old Gloria Steele answered the door. "I'm looking for Charles," the man said.

Just after noon, the young coed's roommate came home to find Steele sprawled out on the bedroom floor in a pool of blood. She had been stabbed to death with a sharp, thin woodcarving tool.

The attack was swift and savage. The killer stabbed Steele between thirty and thirty-five times in the chest and stomach with such force that the shaft of the murder weapon, a woodworker's tool called a skew chisel, was found lodged in her spine. During the frenzy, the handle of the tool became loose and separated from the shaft. Unfortunately, the handle, which may have provided finger-prints and a clue to the identity of Steele's murderer, was gone.

Apart from a piece of the murder weapon, Steele's killer left no other physical evidence at the scene. There was no evidence of sex-ual assault and as a result no semen or hairs. There were no skin particles under Steele's fingernails—she apparently didn't or could-n't fight her assailant. Whoever murdered Gloria Steele attacked quickly and then just left.

Almost two weeks later, Diane K. Williams answered a knock on her apartment door. It was a man asking to see Charles. Williams had seen the man around the apartment complex before, and she thought that perhaps there was a Charles who lived in the vicinity, so she gave him a pen and some paper to leave a note. A few min-utes later, the man came back to Williams's apartment to return the pen and paper.

But when he reached her apartment, he pushed his way through the door and attacked Williams. During the struggle, Williams's phone rang. She managed to kick the phone off the hook and screamed for help. The man bolted, and Williams watched as he got into a tan Pontiac Grand Prix.

Police now had a clue about the mysterious friend of Charles. They tracked the tan Pontiac to Coral Watts and assembled a lineup. Both Lenore Knizacky and Diane K. Williams identified Watts as their attacker. He was arrested on two counts of assault and battery, and during the course of questioning, admitted to fifteen others, but police could not gather enough evidence to charge Watts with Steele's murder.

Watts admitted that he had been at the Stadium Drive complex the day before Steele's murder, but he insisted he had nothing to do with it. Officers searched his room at his parents' home and found woodcarving tools, but since the murder weapon was a common type of tool and the murderer left no other physical evidence at the scene, police had nothing but speculation about Watts's role, if any, in the crime.

Detectives did find some intriguing circumstantial evidence. A parking ticket written for the morning of the Steele murder placed Watts's car across the street from Steele's apartment complex. Watts also said to a Kalamazoo police officer "I guess you have me," and then asked, "Do you have me on all of them?"

Over the next few months, while prosecutors prepared to try him for the two cases of assault and battery, Watts spent time in two different mental health facilities. At the Center for Forensic Psychiatry, Watts told doctors that assaulting women didn't bother him and that he felt good after hurting them. These admissions did not make him unfit to stand trial, though, and in December 1975, Watts faced a judge for the assault and battery of Knizacky and Williams. He pled no contest and was sentenced to a year in the county lockup. Watts did the time and returned to Inkster in August 1976.

In the three years after his release, Coral Watts was involved in two failed relationships. The first relationship—with a childhood friend—ended when Watts abandoned her and the young child they had together. A second relationship led to marriage in August 1979; the newlyweds moved to Detroit, but after just six months, Watts's wife filed for divorce.

Watts made for a strange partner. He had violent nightmares during which he wildly swung his arms, like he was punching something in the air. In addition to this nocturnal shadowboxing, he sliced candles and plants with a knife, threw garbage onto the floor, and disappeared for long periods of time.

What Watts did during these periods of absence has become a topic of interest to cold case investigators. During this phase of Watts's life, a series of unsolved murders and assaults occurred in the greater Detroit area as well as Windsor, Ontario. In the fourteen-month span between October 1979 and November 1980, several women died violent deaths at the hands of an unknown assailant who left little if any physical evidence. Two of the women, Jeanne Clyne and Helen Dutcher, were killed in almost identical circumstances.

Clyne, a former news reporter from Detroit, was walking in her neighborhood on Halloween 1979. In broad daylight and in full view of others, a man walked up to her and jabbed her in the chest and then just walked away. At first, bystanders thought that it was a prank, but when they realized that it was a murder, they called police, who discovered that the forty-four-year-old had been stabbed eleven times.

Five weeks later, a similar slaying occurred a few miles to the east. Helen Dutcher was walking down a dark alley near the intersection of Eight Mile and Woodward when her killer pounced on her and stabbed her twelve times. An eyewitness told police that he saw a man leave the alley and described the suspect to a police sketch artist. This sketch would be a vital piece of evidence against Dutcher's killer—a serial killer who would later become known as the Sunday Morning Slasher.

In 1979, though, the only evidence police had was a sketch of a man seen in a dark alley. Matching the portrait with a name was like finding a needle in a haystack, and the murder remained unsolved.

The murder of young women continued in southeast Michigan, including three committed in the campus town of Ann Arbor. The university hadn't seen such violence since the Coed Killings almost a decade earlier, and this latest rash of homicide once again terrorized residents.

The first of the three victims, seventeen-year-old Shirley Small, was stabbed twice. The second victim, twenty-six-year-old Glenda Richmond, was stabbed twenty-eight times with a stiletto-style weapon like a screwdriver. The third, twenty-year-old Rebecca Huff, was stabbed fifty-four times, also with a screwdriver.

The three Ann Arbor murders were carbon copies of each other. All were women, none were sexually assaulted, all lived alone, and all were murdered around 4 A.M. on Sunday.

About a month after the Sunday Morning Slasher murdered Huff, Ann Arbor police witnessed a strange cat-and-mouse game between a stalker and his intended victim. The woman managed to escape to her apartment, and when the man saw the police, he fled. After a short chase, officers arrested the would-be assailant for driving with a suspended license. The man's name was Coral Watts.

Inside Watts's car, police found woodcarving tools and a collegiate dictionary with the sentence "Rebecca is a lover" carved into its surface. Did the dictionary belong to Rebecca Huff? Was Watts the Sunday Morning Slasher? The pieces fit.

Detectives questioned Watts, but with no direct evidence linking him to the murders, Watts walked after making a phone call. Despite the lack of physical evidence, authorities suspected him and began twenty-four-hour-a-day surveillance. They even placed a transmitter on his car, but Watts knew they were watching. For about four months, they watched every step Coral Watts took. And all of his steps were legal.

At some point, the heat became unbearable. In March 1981, Watts moved to Texas, where he got a job as a mechanic for a transportation company. Over the next few months, Watts changed employers a few times, eventually taking a job working on Houston city buses.

Ann Arbor homicide detective Paul Bunten, who led a task force investigating the Ann Arbor murders, sent Watts's file to Houston police. But Watts was difficult to track. Texas police attempted to keep an eye on him, but he moved several times and often wrote friends' addresses on job applications. The overwhelmed, undermanned Texas authorities just couldn't keep up with Coral Watts.

So despite a paper trail following Watts from Michigan, a series of murders began a few months after he arrived in Texas. But the links of the murder chain remained obscured by the hundreds of homicide files that buried Houston police in the early 1980s. In 1981 alone, the year Watts arrived in Texas, some seven hundred homicides occurred in the Houston area. Police did suspect Watts in some of the cases, but the serial killer's M.O. differed slightly from victim to victim, making it difficult to identify any of the murders as part of a sequence done by the same culprit.

During the first five months of 1982, several young women were murdered in the Houston area. By the spring, the slayings had become an epidemic, so in May 1982, a task force was formed to look into forty unsolved murders of young women in the greater Houston area over the previous two years.

Then in late May, the law finally caught up with the man responsible for a least a dozen of the murders. They apprehended the Sunday Morning Slasher when one of his intended victims foiled a double homicide.

Sometime around two or three o'clock on the morning of Sunday, May 23, Michele Maday was returning home after a night on the town. The night before, she had celebrated her twentieth birthday with friends at an area nightclub. When she arrived at the door of her Houston apartment, she noticed a man behind her and turned, but she didn't have time to scream. The man, Coral Watts, grabbed her neck and squeezed. A few seconds later, Maday was dead.

Watts dragged Maday's lifeless body into the house, filled the bathtub, and dunked the body into the water. Watts later told authorities that he did this to keep her spirit from escaping.

Just a few hours later, Watts attacked two other young women—roommates Lori Lister and Melinda Aguilar. Twenty-one-year-old Lister was returning home from her boyfriend's house around six in the morning. As she reached into her purse for her apartment keys, Watts sneaked up behind her and throttled her. Before Lister lost consciousness, though, she managed to utter a faint cry for help. Watts didn't realize it, but neighbors heard Lister and immediately called the police.

Meanwhile, Watts walked up the stairs to Lister's apartment. Watts was about to enter the apartment when the eighteen-year-old Aguilar heard the jingling of keys. Thinking her roommate had returned, Aguilar approached the door.

Watts, shocked to see a roommate, pounced on Aguilar. "If you scream, I'll kill you," he threatened. Then he began to choke her. Aguilar pretended to pass out, so Watts carried her into one of the bedrooms and set her on the bed.

He returned to the spot where he left Lister lying on the ground. He dragged Lister up the stairs and dropped her on the living room floor. With Lister unconscious on the floor, Watts went back to the bedroom and tied Aguilar's hands behind her back with a wire coat hanger. He then bound Lister's hands and feet with another hanger. Delighted by his two subdued victims, Watts began to jump up and down and clap his hands in joy.

With Aguilar apparently unconscious, Watts dragged Lister to the bathroom, filled the bathtub, and dumped her into it. While Watts attempted to drown Lister in the next room, Aguilar, hands still bound behind her back, tiptoed to the apartment balcony and rolled over the railing. Landing on the ground two stories below, she began to scream for help.

Watts heard Aguilar screaming and ran off, but police arrived moments later and nabbed him as he raced through the apartment courtyard. They had caught the Sunday Morning Slasher in the act.

Both Aguilar and Lister survived and lived to tell about their brush with death. A concerned neighbor pulled Lister out of the bathtub, and the roommates recounted the horrific story to police.

While authorities suspected Watts of multiple murders committed in the Houston area, they did not have the physical evidence needed for a murder conviction, so they made a "deal with the devil," as it has been called in the media. If Watts agreed to plead guilty to burglary with intent to murder Lister and Aguilar—a deal that came with a sentence of sixty years in prison—and provide details about the murders he committed in Texas, they would grant him immunity for those murders. Watts took the deal.

At the time, it seemed like a good deal for authorities. It let Watts off the hook for at least a dozen murders, but it would keep him off of the streets for as long as sixty years, which meant that the twenty-eight-year-old would likely die in prison. And it would bring closure to unresolved murder cases.

Without emotion, Watts gave a lengthy confession. He described twelve murders and five attempted murders he committed in Texas. When asked how he selected his victims, Watts told shocked investigators that he killed women who "had evil in their eyes." Several times during his confession, he repeated the phrase "evil in their eyes."

He would go out at night, he said, and drive around—all night sometimes—until he found a woman with "evil in her eyes." Once he selected his victim, he typically murdered quickly, without hesitation. In some cases, he committed the act in a matter of seconds.

He also said that he felt compelled to get rid of the evil spirits and that he worried about his victims coming back to haunt him, so he sometimes took items like a shoe or a purse and burned them to keep the spirits away.

Some of the victims Watts claimed as his floored investigators. He admitted to murdering twenty-two-year-old Linda Tilley, who was found dead in an apartment swimming pool on September 5, 1981. Police believed Tilley's death was an accidental drowning.

Watts also admitted to assaulting Patty Johnson. On January 30, 1982, a man stabbed the nineteen-year-old in the throat. Johnson survived the attack and later identified the man she thought was her attacker. The man was convicted, but when Watts copped to the crime, Texas authorities realized they had sent the wrong man to prison and freed him.

During his confession, Watts also told police where they could find bodies he'd hidden. He led police to a spot just two hundred yards from the apartment of Suzanne Searles, a twenty-five-year-old woman he murdered in late April. Watts told investigators that he forced her head into a flowerpot filled with water, drowned her, and then buried the body.

Watts watched police unearth Searles's remains. While they labored in the intense heat, he calmly asked for a hamburger, fries, and a Coke. If they didn't get him a hamburger, he threatened, he wouldn't take them to any more graves.

Watts got his hamburger and the police another grave. He led investigators to the spot where he buried Carrie Jefferson. Watts attacked the thirty-two-year-old on the morning of April 16, 1982. He throttled her, threw her body into the trunk of her own car, and drove to an open field. As he dug a grave, he heard her kicking in the trunk and realized that he hadn't killed her. So he opened the trunk, choked her again, and then stabbed her in the neck before burying her body.

The Sunday Morning Slasher also committed an untold number of crimes in Michigan, leaving file cabinets bulging with unsolved crimes. To clear one entry in the books, the prosecutor's office of Michigan's Wayne County offered Watts immunity in exchange for a statement about the murder of Jeanne Clyne. So in addition to the twelve Texas murders, Watts confessed to murdering Clyne in Gross Pointe Farms on Halloween 1979, bringing his admitted total to thirteen. He said that he had spotted her walking down the sidewalk. He walked up to her, pulled a screwdriver from his sweatshirt, and repeatedly stabbed her in the chest.

He offered to confess to additional murders in Ann Arbor, Detroit, and Kalamazoo, Michigan (as well as Ontario, Canada), but Michigan prosecutors would not swap immunity for confessions, so Watts stopped talking. Dozens of cases that now appeared to be his work remained open.

During his confession, Watts made a chilling admission. "If I get out," he said, "I'm going to kill again." But thanks to Texas authorities, even though Watts got away with murder, his plea bargain would keep him safely behind bars for a long, long time.

Or would it? Coral Watts went to prison, but a technicality in his case changed everything. The judge who presided over the plea bargain entered a finding that the bathtub water Watts used in an attempt to drown Lori Lister constituted a deadly weapon. The use of a deadly weapon classified Watts as a violent offender and prevented him from earning days off of his sentence with good conduct.

Then in 1987, the Texas Court of Criminal Appeals made a ruling that threatened to make the Sunday Morning Slasher a free man. The court ruled that criminals have a right to know if the judge plans to make a ruling that would prevent them from receiving good conduct time. In other words, criminals were entitled to prior notice that a deadly weapons finding, which would eliminate good conduct time, would be made.

The presiding judge did not provide prior notice about his deadly weapon finding, so Watts was reclassified as a non-violent offender. Under Texas law at the time, first-time, non-violent offenders received an incentive for serving time without incident. For each day inside, they received three days off of their sentence. This legal loophole reduced Watts's sentence by thirty-five years, which would make him a free man in 2006 and the first American serial killer to be released from prison. Although Watts said that he would kill again if he went free, Texas law handcuffed police who blanched at the thought of Watts back on the prowl.

But there was a chance to keep Watts behind bars. With the exception of the Clyne case, Michigan authorities had not traded information for immunity. They now had an opportunity to prosecute Watts for murder in Michigan, and more importantly, keep him in prison for the rest of his life—if they could make a case against him.

This was a big "if." They needed concrete evidence tying Watts to one of his victims, but Watts didn't leave much physical evidence at the crime scenes. Perhaps they could find an eyewitness. Watts said that he was willing to make a deal and confess to several Michigan murders, and investigators considered him a prime suspect in as many as ninety open cases in the Great Lakes State. If he committed only a fraction of that number, someone somewhere must have seen something. Investigators reopened files that had lay dormant for twenty years and searched for evidence.

The break they needed came from a phone call. The eyewitness who saw Watts flee the scene of the Dutcher murder called police after he saw a television spot asking potential witnesses to come forward if they might know something about Watts's crimes. The man, a Detroit-area resident named Joseph Foy, contacted the Ferndale police in 1979 and gave a description to a sketch artist, but the investigation stalled. Now, Foy became the key witness in the state's case against Watts for the 1979 murder of Helen Dutcher.

With enough evidence to make a case in the Dutcher murder, Michigan governor Jennifer Granholm requested extradition, and

Texas governor Rick Perry quickly signed the papers. Coral Watts was headed for a Michigan courtroom.

The trial began in November 2004. Watts, who had begun a long battle with prostate cancer, fidgeted nervously as the prosecution presented its case.

On the second day of the trial, Foy took the stand. He said he was sitting on his back porch when Helen Dutcher was attacked and murdered, and he described in detail the scene he witnessed. The prosecution then presented the 1979 sketch of the perpetrator alongside a period photograph of Watts. The two images matched.

Watts's defense attempted to discredit Foy's description by pointing out that Foy was possibly eighty feet away from a scene that occurred in a dimly lit alley. The jury, though, believed Foy. Nine days after the trial began, they returned their verdict. Watts was guilty of first-degree murder and sentenced to life in prison without the possibility of parole.

Michigan prosecutors wanted to take out an insurance policy to ensure that Watts, even if freed on appeal by some legal technicality, would never go free. So they prepared to try Watts for the 1974 murder of Gloria Steele.

Watts's second Michigan murder trial began on July 25, 2007. To illustrate his modus operandi, the prosecution introduced evidence of four additional murders—two in Texas and two in Ann Arbor—that were virtual carbon copies of the Steele murder. It took only two days for prosecutors to convince the jury, who returned another guilty verdict. Along with the verdict came another life sentence, ensuring that Watts would spend the rest of his life behind bars.

Life in a Michigan prison would only last a few years for Coral Watts. On September 21, 2007, he succumbed to prostate cancer at the age of fifty-three, leaving many, many unanswered questions.

Just how many victims did Watts murder? He confessed to thirteen, was convicted of two more, and at one point offered to tell Michigan authorities about several others, but only in exchange for immunity.

After Watts made the deal with Texas prosecutors in 1981, Ann Arbor homicide detective Paul Bunten traveled to Texas and interviewed Watts in prison. Ann Arbor authorities didn't plea bargain with Watts, who would only confess with a deal on the table. So Watts didn't admit to the three Ann Arbor murders, but he did tell Bunten that he could stop looking for the killer.

The total number may never be clear, because not only did Watts choose his victims at random and leave virtually no evidence at the crime scenes, he also used different methods. On some occasions, he stabbed his victims, sometimes with screwdrivers and sometimes with other weapons. He also throttled, drowned, and even hanged victims. And unlike many other serial killers, he never raped them, which would have left crucial forensic evidence that could be tested for DNA and bring closure to unsolved murders.

While many murder cases linked to Coral Watts remain officially unsolved, Michele Maday's epitaph leaves little doubt about her fate. Her gravestone reads, "Murdered by Coral Eugene Watts"

How many other gravestones could say the same thing remains a mystery.

# Bibliography

"Arrest in Peck Poison Plot Mystery Is Expected within Next 48 Hours." *Grand Rapids Herald*, March 23, 1916.

Bernstein, Arnie. *Bath Massacre: America's First School Bombing*. Ann Arbor: University of Michigan Press, 2009.

Brandt, Charles. *I Heard You Paint Houses: Frank "The Irishman" Sheeran and the Inside Story of the Mafia, the Teamsters, and the Last Ride of Jimmy Hoffa*. Hanover, NH: Steerforth Press, 2005.

Brown, Wenzell. *Introduction to Murder: The Unpublished Facts Behind the Notorious Lonely Hearts Killers, Martha Beck and Raymond Fernandez*. New York: Greenburg, 1952.

Burton, Clarence Monroe, William Stocking, and Gordon K. Miller. *The City of Detroit, Michigan, 1701–1922*. Detroit-Chicago: S. J. Clarke, 1922.

Carlo, Philip. *The Ice Man: Confessions of a Mafia Contract Killer*. New York: St. Martin's Press, 2006.

Catlin, George. *The Story of Detroit*. Detroit: Detroit News, 1923.

"Crime: The Rainy Day Murders." *Time*, August 8, 1969.

Deney, Margrete. "Killer's Skull to Be Studied." *Toledo Blade*, May 23, 1927.

Dodge, Roy. *Michigan Ghost Towns, Vol. 2*. Troy, MI: Glendon Publishing, 1993.

———. *Ticket to Hell: A Saga of Michigan's Bad Men*. Tawas City, MI: Northeastern Printers, 1975.

Ellsworth, M. J., and Jean Martin. *The Bath School Disaster*. Bath, MI: Bath School Museum Committee, 1991.

Farmer, Silas. *The History of Detroit and Michigan*. Detroit: S. Farmer, 1884.

"FBI Ends Search for Jimmy Hoffa's Body at Detroit Farm." Associated Press, May 30, 2006.

**137**

Fitzpatrick, Doyle C. *The King Strang Story: A Vindication of James J. Strang, the Beaver Island Mormon King.* Lansing, MI: National Heritage, 1970.

Flesher, John. "Police Come Up Empty in Jimmy Hoffa Investigation." Associated Press, July 17, 2003.

Gilbert, Bill. "America's only king made Beaver Island his Promised Land." *Smithsonian*, August 1, 1995.

Hoffman, William, and Lake Headley. *Contract Killer: The Explosive Story of the Mafia's Most Notorious Hitman, Donald "Tony the Greek" Frankos.* New York: Thunder's Mouth Press, 1992.

"The Hunt for Hoffa Heats Up." *Detroit Free Press*, May 19, 2006.

"Hunt Purple Chiefs in Hijack Massacre," *The Detroit Times*, September 17, 1931.

James, Earl. *Catching Serial Killers: Learning from Past Serial Murder Investigations.* Lansing, MI: International Forensics Services, 1991.

Kavieff, Paul. *The Purple Gang: Organized Crime in Detroit 1910–1945.* Fort Lee, NJ: Barricade Books, 2000.

Keyes, Edward. *The Michigan Murders.* New York: Reader's Digest, 1976.

Leung, Rebecca. "A Deal with the Devil?" *60 Minutes*, October 14, 2004.

"Levine's Story of Massacre Checked." *The Detroit Times*, November 3, 1931.

"Lonely Hearts Pair Confess 3 Slayings." *Grand Rapids Herald*, March 2, 1949.

"Maniac Blows Up School." *New York Times*, May 19, 1927.

Mitchell, Corey. *Evil Eyes: The Most Insatiable Serial Killer Ever.* New York: Kensington, 2006.

Moore, Charles. *The History of Michigan.* Chicago: Lewis Publishing, 1915.

Moore, Evan. "DREAMS/Coral Eugene Watts Murdered at Least 13 Women, but Went to Prison Only for Aggravated Burglary; Someday, He'll Get Out." *Houston Chronicle*, April 7, 1991.

"Murdered Two, Tried for a Third, Waite Tells Jury." *New York Times*, May 26, 1916.

"'Other Woman' Turns Wife from Dr. Waite." *New York Times*, March 26, 1916.

*People of the State of Michigan v. Coral Eugene Watts*, State of Michigan Court of Appeals Unpublished Opinion, April 25, 2006.

*People of the State of Michigan v. Coral Eugene Watts*, State of Michigan Court of Appeals Unpublished Opinion, August 8, 2006.

*People of the State of Michigan v. Gary Earl Leiterman*, State of Michigan Court of Appeals Unpublished Opinion, July 24, 2007.

Powers, Tom. *Michigan Rogues, Desperados, and Cut-Throats: A Gallery of 19th Century Miscreants.* Davison, MI: Thunder Bay Press, 2004.

"Pretty Teacher Trapped Waite." *New York Times*, May 25, 1916.

Reimann, Lewis. *Incredible Seney: the Complete Story of Michigan's Fabulous Lumber Town.* AuTrain, MI: Avery Color Studios, 1989.

Repetto, Thomas. *Bringing Down the Mob: The War against the American Mafia.* New York: Henry Holt and Company, 2006.

"Report Purple Gang Smashed." *The Reading (PA) Eagle*, June 30, 1935.

Rockaway, Robert. *But he was Good to his Mother: The Lives and Crimes of Jewish Gangsters.* New York: Gefen, 2000.

Russell, Thaddeus. *Out of the Jungle: Jimmy Hoffa and the Remaking of the American Working Class.* New York: Knopf, 2001.

"School Dynamiter First Slew Wife." *New York Times*, May 20, 1927.

"See Waite in Plot to Kill Many More." *New York Times*, March 26, 1916.

Shepardson, David. "Hit Man: Hoffa Is in Junked Car." *Detroit News*, April 18, 2006.

"Shot in the Head." *The Diamond Drill* (Crystal Falls, MI), December 5, 1891.

Silbar, Howard. "Michigan's Poisoning Maniac." *Detective Files* (March 1978): 21–45.

"Slayers Waive Court Hearing; Trail Traced Across Country." *Grand Rapids Press*, March 2, 1949.

Sloan, Arthur. *Hoffa*. Cambridge, MA: MIT Press, 1991.

State of Michigan. *In the Matter of the Inquest as to the Cause of Death of Emery C. Huyck*, May 23, 1927.

"2 Slayers May Face Chair." *Grand Rapids Herald*, March 3, 1949.

Van Noord, Roger. *Assassination of a Michigan King: The Life of James Jesse Strang.* Ann Arbor: University of Michigan Press, 2000.

"Waite Confesses to Two Murders." *New York Times*, March 29, 1916.

"Waite Now Admits Intent to Kill Wife." *New York Times*, April 3, 1916.

Wakefield, Larry. *Ghost Towns of Michigan*. West Bloomfield, MI: Northmont, 1994.

Whitley, Glenna. "Evil Eyes: Coral Eugene Watts is a Serial Killer. He Says He'll Murder Again. Why Can't Texas Stop Him?" *Dallas Observer*, June 19, 2003.

# *Other Titles in the*
# True Crime Series